£5.95

COME BACK AT TWO

by

Sheelagh Warren

A description of life in Uganda
between 1957 and 1990

COME BACK AT TWO

by
Sheelagh Warren

Excalibur Press of London
4-6 Effie Road, London SW6 1TD

Copyright © 1993 Sheelagh Warren

Illustrations by Christina Kasozimusoke

Printed and bound in the UK
Published by Excalibur Press of London
ISBN 1 85634 214 X

FOREWORD

There is a Steinbeck novel about Africa in which the old hand tries to pacify the exasperated newcomer. "It's not violence which will drive you out of Africa; it's the frustrations." Sheelagh had plenty of both, but never gave up. This is her story, written with humour, gentleness and patience, describing how over thirty years at Gayaza High School, they experienced the Lord's enabling and protection time and time again.

Sheelagh writes from two viewpoints: *first* as an expatriate mission partner learning to understand the life and culture of Ugandan people, making friendships, appreciating their joy and spontaneity. Her professional contribution to girls' education was known and respected by all from the most junior pupil to top officials in the Ministry of Education.

Second, as one born in Kigezi, Sheelagh was never an outsider. She writes of shared plans, dreams, disappointments and triumphs. She agonized over the collapse and destruction of the country and the loss of so many friends. She prayed and worked for its restoration and return to peace, and still does. Her Ugandan colleagues were also her friends. Gayaza was not only a school, it was her home.

CMS has had a long association with Sheelagh's family. Her grandparents and parents were distinguished missionaries before her; her doctor mother courageously continued work in Uganda after the early death of her father. Her uncle, Max Warren, was an outstanding General Secretary of the Society. Few such family networks now remain in mission service. The benefits in terms of understanding, prayer support and encouragement were great. This is Sheelagh's story but more than that, it is a wonderful account of the grace of God, enjoyed, experienced and lived out in every circumstance.

Rev Christopher L Carey
CMS Overseas Regional Secretary, East Africa

CONTENTS

COME BACK AT TWO   1

Introduction and historical note   4
1   Praise him, shining star   9
2   Train up a child   17
3   Going out and coming in   27
4   Never Give Up   39
5   Not many mighty are called   49
6   Loaves and fishes   57
7   In the presence of my enemies   67
8   Sing a new song   81
9   Be faithful unto death   91
10   My cup overflows   99

COME BACK AT TWO

Miss Warren went to the Ministry
To see an officer she wanted to see:
"He's just gone out but he'll be back soon;
Why don't you come back in the afternoon?"
"Come back at two," they told her. "Come back at two.
Come back at two, and if not, tomorrow will do."

Miss Warren went to the Water Board:
"We've got no water and there's nothing stored."
"The man you want is not around:
He's gone to Gaba and he can't be found.
"Come back at two," they told her. "Come back at two.
Come back at two and if not, tomorrow will do."

Miss Warren went to the UEB:
"We've got no lights again and we can't see.
"Exams are on; there's FA 1 to weigh."
"But the line to Bombo isn't working today..."
"Come back at two," they told her........

Miss Warren went in to UNEB:
"There's a paper short, and no music tape.
Results are missing and I'll get no peace;
And we've got no money to pay the police."
"Come back at two," they told her...

Miss Warren went to select S. One
Lots of Old Girls wanted daughters to come.

"She put Budo first and she got a '4';
I was out of the country, just squeeze in one more!"
"Don't come at two, dear parents; don't come at two;
Don't come at two because there is no place for you!"

Miss Warren went to the HMA;
She had lots of things she wanted to say.
Nobody came in over two hours:
Then she found the meeting wasn't in Crested Towers!
"Come back at two," they told her. "Come back at two.....

Our love goes with you as you leave us here;
We hope the future will be bright and clear.
Return to visit us one fine day.
There's only one thing that is left to say:
"Come back at two, dear Sheelagh, come back at two.
Come back at any time, we'll be waiting for you."

An ad hoc song late at night at my farewell with the staff of Gayaza, where I lived and taught from 1957 to 1990, gives as clear an explanation as any of the title of this book. I was HM for eighteen of those years, and life was indeed a series of abortive attempts to get simple practical things done. In later years, no one said, "Come back at two," any longer, because no one had money for lunch. They worked on until they finished for the day and went home for supper.

This book is a tribute to them all: schoolgirls, teachers, administrative and compound staff, government officials, police officers, market-stall holders, parents and servants. We all knew what it was like to be told:

He's not here...There isn't any...The line is out of order...no money...no water...no petrol...no sugar...and perhaps worst of all:

NO PLACE

For a place in a good secondary school for one's child was the one thing worth hoping for when the rest of the world was falling apart.

I can't promise to be back at two, but I'll be back sometime, for I left my heart there.

HISTORICAL NOTE:

Speke discovered the Source of the Nile at Jinja, Uganda in 1861; the Anglican Church was established in 1877 and the Roman Catholic in 1879, and Uganda remained a British Protectorate until its Independence in 1962 when Sir Edward Mutesa, King of Buganda, became President, and Milton Obote, a northerner, became the first Prime Minister.

This compromise did not work, and within three years Obote seized power and the President fled to the UK. A reign of terror began for the central tribe, the Baganda, and certain elements in the army began to revolt. While Obote was in Singapore at the Commonwealth Conference in January 1971, General Idi Amin carried out an almost silent coup, which he followed up by bringing back the body of the former President, Sir Edward Mutesa for a state burial, which of course made him popular with the Baganda.

For a time things seemed better, but Amin had no idea of economics, and his advisers were military men. He declared an 'Economic War' and expelled all the Asians in ninety days at the end of 1972. From then until he was toppled in turn by a Tanzanian army in 1979, there was chaos in the country. Not only did all the economic benefits disappear, but a regime of torture began and many of the professional people fled or were murdered. After the 1979 Liberation there were several short term presidents, but in 1980 Obote was back and held elections which were clearly rigged against the potential opposition. This led to a number of intellectuals and some army officers taking to the bush. Another set of reprisals followed and thousands more were killed, especially in the Luwero Triangle where the guerrillas were operating. People there either had to flee, join primitive survival camps, or die. Hundreds of thousands died, and the whole area, one of the most agriculturally productive, was devastated.

The atrocities shocked the world and the guerrilla leader, Yoweri Museveni, gradually gained support. There were several coups in 1985, and desperate attempts at peace talks until January 1986 when the present Republic was born. Even then rebellious groups in the North and East, probably inspired and supported by the ousted presidents, fought the new government, but Museveni established himself and slowly began to address the multitudinous problems that had accumulated, with much of the country's infrastructure ruined.

There were no good roads, few telephones working, factories and hospitals and even schools had been looted or destroyed. Most means of transport were out-dated; farmers had no machinery; shops were empty; supplies of food were scarce, and no development had taken place. The idea of a newspaper free to express opinions other than those of the government, had almost disappeared. There was an enormous amount to do on every front, and there were thousands of orphans and homeless people wandering about.

Slowly, things began to look up; the idea of democracy was revived; a few businesses began to flourish; parents realised that schools could not survive on meaningless grants and PTA's began fund-raising; the World Food Programme was able to help children to be fed adequately at school; doctors and others returned from well-paid overseas posts and hospitals began to provide service - though bribery and corruption had crept into all fields since the troubles began. Roads were tarmacked, boreholes sunk, taxi and bus services were restored and some of the

Asians who had been driven out by Amin were recalled and came back to rehabilitate their ruined factories.

In the midst of all this, schools went on. Ours was only a few miles from the Luwero Triangle, but the impact seldom hit us. We had armed men crossing our compound; we had to pass up to six road blocks to reach the bank or the ministry; we had no telephone for ten years and very unreliable transport; water and electricity supplies were very erratic; we lost staff at a moment's notice when their lives were threatened; our road became almost impassable in wet weather.

Almost, but not quite... The children never missed a meal. The school never closed. We became a refuge for many who had nowhere else safe to sleep. We also stayed near the top of the league table for exam results and other competitions. We went on because we had to, and we looked back in amazement at what we had been able to survive, thanks to the determination of all our members, and the loving mercy of God.

This little book is an attempt to describe the country in its beauty as well as its horrors, and to show how gracious and resilient its people proved in the face of so much disaster. When I began to run a school I spent a lot of time calling on officials, since the telephone wires had been looted and all business had to be done in person. Very often I was greeted with the news that the man I wanted wasn't there and told to "Come back at two". That meant either going without lunch or paying the earth for it, so it was not advice they expected to be taken. In the end when one got home with nothing to report, one had only to say, "Come back at two," and the reason was well understood. What the reader might not realise is that every journey of ten miles was an adventure, risking at worst a hold-up, at least a puncture or finding no petrol at the garage; and the road was all potholes, so it was no joy-ride. I came to regard forty minutes in the classroom as a luxury by comparison. There it was cool and quiet and one had some measure of control.

And what about the church? It is there as everywhere in the Anglican Communion with all the structures of parishes and dioceses, and beside the Anglican the Catholics, Orthodox, Baptists, Pentecostals and a myriad sects. But the real church is wherever believers gather to worship God together, and as things became more difficult the real church could be found anywhere, any time, crossing the boundaries that usually divide people, and witnessing to the love and lordship of Christ in all circumstances. When things were dark the Protestants and Catholics stood together. It was only when peace came back that the divisions reared their heads again. And now the problems remain: rebuilding confidence as well as infrastructures, and coping with the thousands of Aids sufferers and the orphans they leave behind. But there is no doubt that Ugandans will manage somehow, for they never give up.

1. PRAISE HIM SHINING STARS

When people say, "Thirty-three years in Uganda! Aren't you homesick?" the first things that flash across my memory are the people themselves, set against their background of bright green grass and trees, flashing kingfishers and raucous ibises, clear blue skies and red-brown murram roads - colourful, vibrant, cheerful and welcoming.

I was born in Uganda, but taken home when still a baby, and the Eastern district where I lived briefly at the age of seven was very different from Buganda, where I spent nearly all my days from 1957 to 1990. I was met off a small thirty-four seater plane at Entebbe by a landrover full of third-year students from the school, and these were to be my first class - just fifteen of them, so we got to know each other well. When I left, at least three of them had daughters in the school, one of whom became headgirl. But she cannot have been as fierce or determined a prefect as her mother had been: she used to keep the teachers in order too. When I was new she would stand in my path and say, "I'm Lydia," in a tone which suggested that I had better know her next day. Of course I did, and we remained good friends long after she left.

Nothing can be more beautiful or dignified than the Baganda ladies' national dress, the busuuti or gomesi. As a school we claim to have invented it, because the original dress for ladies was just a long piece of cloth tied under the armpits. When the famous Miss Allen, who walked up from the coast and founded the school in 1905, saw this costume she immediately designed a yoke for it; and the local tailor, Mr Gomez, put the new garment together, which being worn by the first girls in a boarding school was nicknamed the "bordingi". A proper dress takes six yards of material, most of which is loosely pleated and falls from the waist, the garment being held up by a magnificent sash about eight inches wide, tied in a reef knot below the waist. Quite a lot is worn underneath, and the larger the lady looks the more respect she will be accorded; thinness is not admired in Uganda. The Mothers' Union wear a white busuuti with a blue sash as their uniform; Gayaza Old Girls wear white with red, and every Ugandan woman aspires to wear the costume as soon as she marries, if not before. Old ones are worn for digging and funerals; splendid new ones, cotton or nylon in any bright floral print for weddings and parties, and the wearers look really majestic.

One's first sight of Uganda from the air is of Lake Victoria, the size of Wales and the source of the Nile, home of a good many crocodiles and plentiful supply of fish, Nile perch and tilapia in particular. Most of the fishermen cannot swim, but swimming is only safe right by the shore, and even there you risk bilharzia. A good tarmac road runs the twenty miles from the airport to Kampala, and the visitor is bound to notice especially the banana trees with their single bunch of fruit, usually the plantain, which is eaten green and is the chief diet of the Baganda. As a food it is mostly water and not good for babies, who often suffer from kwashiorkor as a result of being given it too young. The deep red-brown of the murram soil also catches the attention, and on a good day the clarity of the air, with flowers blazing against the deep blue of the sky. As night falls, the stars, undimmed by street lights and sharply etched against the dark sky, seeming much nearer and brighter than in Europe, give great joy.

"Praise him, shining stars!" says Psalm 8. The stars in Uganda certainly lift the heart to God. I often fell over in the dark through walking along gazing at the stars, and to cover my confusion if a nightwatchman happened to see me would say, "Look!". But they saw nothing unusual or remarkable up there and could only think I must have seen a thief or a snake. They did get excited by Halley's Comet, especially when they found some of us tramping through the dew at four a.m. to get a look at it; and the youngest children on the compound expressed their determination to live for another seventy-six years to see it again. "God is great!" the old men admitted that time.

January to March can be very dry, dusty and hot, but when the rains come in March the whole earth seems to breathe the same thankfulness that human beings feel. Farmers are only interested in their crops, but for me the freshness was an ever-recurring marvel. Hopkins wrote, "There lives the dearest freshness deep down things," and those words came back to me many times as I looked out on the bright shining grass in the morning, the dart of a woodland kingfisher, the stalking heron on the lookout for a breakfast snake, the yellow cassia blossom against the sky and the magical light in the evening which caught the lilies underneath and shone through them, making them almost transparent. The moon was bigger there, too, and right overhead when it was full, and so bright that you could see the colours of people's clothes and even read a letter by its light.

Not everything was so clean and beautiful: a journey in dry weather takes you past trees so coated with dust that they are no longer green, and in the wet season the way mud sticks to everything you wonder people don't use it for paint. In a way they do, because the basic homestead is made of upright poles filled in with mud and plastered with mud too, and then thatched with grass. Along all the roads people sell the containers and utensils they have make from plants and trees and clay: beautiful objects, many of which find their way back as decorations in European homes, and yet so useful for carrying food, or fetching and storing water, beer or milk.

There is a price for all this beauty, and when a storm strikes anything can happen, from a broken bridge to a roof torn off and blown yards away, a fallen tree, a swollen river bursting its banks, crops washed away and goats struck by lightning. The road you came on, perhaps to visit a school in the bush which is nevertheless putting students in for O level, is suddenly a road no longer, but a rushing torrent, or a series of deep ruts which an ordinary car can hardly negotiate, or a deep bed of mud which sucks the tyres into itself and leaves you well and truly stuck. The locals know that and immediately appear from everywhere only too willing to push - for a price - and if the operation takes some minutes extra help will arrive, and you may find twenty claiming to have rescued you, when three of four could easily have managed. In the depths of the countryside not many cars will need rescuing like that, so the opportunity must not be missed.

"If the buffalo comes towards you, lie down until it has passed," said old Mrs Wilson, whose family had brought us on a buffalo hunt. The trouble was that the grass was about ten feet high and we couldn't see anything but the path we were making through it. Just then we came to a clearing with a tall anthill in the middle and instinctively we women rushed towards it and got off the path. There was a lot of excited shouting: "There! There!" and shots rang out, and in a moment quiet again and we began to think of climbing down. I couldn't move: my knees had turned to jelly. In the end we were all reunited, and went to view the carcass, whose meat was to be our diet for the next three days - the hunters were serious and had not brought any other food. Sadly, the animal was a female in calf, which they would not have shot if they had seen it clearly. I have seldom seen anything lovelier than that embryo, nearly ready to be born, and perfect in every detail, only its hooves were still soft.

Ugandan wildlife is wonderful, all the more so to me for having seen most of its species by chance or at least not as a tourist. In the days before Amin's men plundered the game parks, elephants had right of way, there were notices to say so, and they needed to be respected. On the same trip as the buffalo expedition, since the grass was too high to have any chance of hunting elephant, we went into the park, having buried the guns outside. As we were returning to the ferry near the exit towards dusk, we came upon an elephant peacefully cropping the weeds in the middle of the road, although there was lush grass at the roadside. Nothing that anyone did could persuade Jumbo to move, and there we sat helpless until eventually she tired of the game and ambled off. We raced to the ferry - "Too late," we were told.

"But we are day visitors, not sleeping in the park." After a while someone did ferry us out, only it was even harder to persuade the men on the gate to let us go. In the dark some warthogs went scurrying across our path, tails waving like flags, but we encountered no more elephants that day.

The best view of birds is from a motor launch, but the first time I tried that, I had twelve teenagers aboard who were screaming with excitement at being on water for the first time, and refused to believe that the birds were flying off for fear of them. Dozens of species could be seen on the shore and crocodiles and hippos in abundance as well. Loveliest of all is the fish eagle, a truly majestic bird with an imperious call, flashing white against sky and lake, and he can be seen at Entebbe a few yards from the airport. So can the monkeys, colobus and others, who arrive in families at dawn on Mondays to get the leftovers from the weekend picnics.

Children always ask about snakes. I have seen a python as thick if not as long as a telegraph pole; I have encountered a snake coiled round a loo seat when camping near the Lake; I have had them fall down my chimney in the middle of supper, and found them on the verandah quite often. But the most alarming encounter was the one I found lying along the door sill at night when I was alone in the house. I jumped over it, only to realise that all means of killing it were the other side of the door, so it was necessary to jump back over it. It had to be done, and the snake, still asleep, had to be sacrificed to my peace of mind, in case it came to join me in bed. They say that few snakes in Uganda are dangerous, but they strike terror into the hearts of all so they usually get killed. They say people die of fright, rather than the bite, and I can believe it. There is a kind of primitive revulsion one feels towards them that is not in keeping with D H Lawrence's reverence for "one of the lords of life". I would never visit a snake park.

I had no trouble with spiders, for in Uganda spiders trap mosquitoes so must be considered friendly, along with geckos, which have transparent stomachs, enabling one to watch the process of digestion. In some ways our most dreaded species were ants, because they destroy so much so quickly. Safari ants just terrorise - walk into their path and you will be screeching with pain as you tug them off your toes, to which they stick like leeches. Dogs get frantic when they make that mistake. Then there are the minute ones that swarm into kitchens and take possession of your larder, completely covering anything edible and so fragile that you inevitably squash them in the process of trying to get rid of them. But white ants are the worst. They come up through the floor, out of the walls or the ceiling, pushing the mud of the bricks they have broken all over whatever is in their path. They can ruin a shelf of books, reams of paper, bales of material, planks of wood - anything that is softer than metal or concrete. They always go for your most expensive books, your most recently painted piece of wall and the middle of a ream of paper, and it takes them only a few minutes to do pounds worth of irreparable damage. I lived in an old mission house built in 1908, and I used to reckon it was held up by ants. They certainly made it clear that it was their domain long before it was mine. Clearing up the results of a foray by white ants at midnight became one of my less relished occupations, and it was essential to move things that you did not use often, like trunks and cases, or you were likely to find they had been quietly invaded in your absence.

Away from Uganda, one looks back with nostalgia, missing the sunshine and forgetting the intense wearing heat of the dry season; recalling the brilliance of the stars and forgetting the mosquitoes; regretting the freedom of wearing few and bright clothes and forgetting the jiggers in one's toes; recalling the excitement and fury of thunderstorms, and forgetting how often one's cherished flowers and vegetables were destroyed in a minute. To love Uganda you need to come to terms with a place which is more colourful and vibrant than Europe, but a lot more demanding of resilience; and resilience is the quality I remember best in the people. Their world could be shattered by sudden and violent deaths, by total destruction of their property, by loss of positions of authority overnight when a new regime came in, or simply by storm and flood and fire. Our school anthem, drawn mainly from Psalm 107, urges us to:

> *Give thanks to the Lord because he is good;*
> *His love is eternal.*
> *In peace and war, in fire and flood,*
> *His love is eternal.*

And it ends:

> *Now and forever He'll hold you fast:*
> *His love is eternal, so never give up.*

If this book had a subtitle it would be "Never Give Up" - not so much to urge the reader that way, but to affirm that this is the spirit of Ugandans, especially of those who know that God's love is eternal. They have a perspective on life which is uncomplaining and accepting, which sees impossibility becoming possible: "What is impossible with man is possible with God" - that was the family song of our bishop, and it wasn't a pious wish but something born of experience. We all used to find that trusting God proved over and over again to be the only way to live; and when you did, anything could happen, as the rest of this book shows.

2. TRAIN UP A CHILD

A few months after the last Liberation War, when President Yoweri Museveni took over, I visited the Luwero Triangle, escorted by an elderly policeman, a social worker, and the Archdeacon. After reporting our presence to the remains of the police station, we set off in a landrover along what used to be roads and came into a clearing where there was a church and a primary school. The walls of the church were daubed with obscene slogans, and all the furniture had been removed and used for firewood by the avenging soldiers. The school had the remains of five or six classrooms, but most had no doors or window-frames, none had a roof and again the furniture had been looted. All there was to show it was a school was a blackboard still painted on the wall, but the students were there. The senior twelve-year-olds were sitting on a pile of bricks, sometimes with a plank on more bricks as a makeshift desk; the younger ones were on the floor.

"Have all the pupils returned?" I asked.

"Not all, but as soon as they have any clothes at all to wear, they come back."

Those children would in November sit the same examination to qualify for a leaving certificate as their friends in Kampala, who had not really known about this war and who sat at desks in tidy uniforms and were brought to school and fetched by car.

The spirit of never give up - one school's motto - characterises the general attitude of all involved in education. Considering the shortages of textbooks and teachers, the lack of basic facilities, let alone chemicals or paints, it should have been impossible for most schools to continue, but less than a month after the end of the 1979 war the secondary headmasters were all assembled in a leaking building in Kampala to select the students who would begin their new courses in a few weeks' time, ready to regale the company with tales of how their vehicles had been looted, their supplies stolen, their houses attacked, their students scattered, but assuming that education would go on, no matter what. And it did go on, and when we were still tied to Kenya by the same O level exams Uganda did even better, even without equipment, and despite the fact that hundreds of teachers defected across the border for political or economic reasons.

Ugandans have a passion for education and the desire of parents to get their children the best led to many abuses of the system. Young children of four or five would be in the city till 6.00pm being coached for entry to primary one; young teenagers would be called back to school on Saturday and Sunday to make sure they passed the PLE with a good enough grade to be admitted to one of the ten top schools for their secondary education; teachers, desperately trying to survive on pathetic salaries, would do private coaching and give preferential treatment to those who attended the extra classes, so that even parents who disliked coaching found it hard to keep their children away; and even students at the best schools would spend their holidays being coached by university professors for their O and A level exams, because the professors didn't have enough to live on either.

All this made school administration something of a nightmare, because the endless queues of hopeful parents at the office throughout the first weeks of every term got little joy, and the pressures exerted on head teachers to admit unsuitable candidates who were related to someone in authority, or whose sponsors even offered bribes, were extremely wearing.

Somehow the task was accomplished, and eventually the shining students would find their way to Makerere University, complete a degree course with little more in the way of facilities than they had had at school, and go out to perform miracles themselves in some professional post. And fifteen years later they would be back on the doorstep with a young girl also seeking admission, and by then facing far greater competition than her parents did.

However much parents shouted at headteachers about places, fees, pocket money and exeats there was no doubt that they valued their services and headteachers certainly deserved the respect most of them enjoyed. A typical day could include an assembly for the whole school, followed by dealing with a discipline problem. This would be interrupted by some crisis on the compound or the farm, like the cutting down of the wrong tree, or sick animals needing the vet when the transport was out and the telephone out of order. Mid-morning one would go to the town, twelve miles away, to solve a problem of immigration or registration. To save time, the driver would be sent on another ploy and get himself arrested for some trumped-up offence by a policeman hoping for a bribe. When at last you were reunited, tired and hungry, you might go to the market and stock up with food, even fish or meat for the weekend, and arrive back at school to find that the heavy rain during the afternoon had put the electricity and therefore the fridge out of action, as well as the lights; and for sure there would be a parent waiting at the office with a new problem between you and a cup of tea; and a message to say that a sick child needed taking home, her temperature giving cause for alarm, so the driver wouldn't get his tea either. After that, while it was still possible to see, the letters had to be opened, the problems that had arisen for the staff or prefects dealt with, and supper to be cooked on a "sigiri" - a charcoal stove which had to be tended throughout the cooking process. Bread and cheese were rare luxuries, so one had to cook a meal.

The underlying problem was always finance: we lived from hand to mouth, and when the auditors came and finally told you that you were within the budget by a few shillings, it was a miracle.

The secret of managing was to have a good staff, a devoted Board of Governors and an enterprising Parent-Teachers Association. With those at your side and at your back you could survive, and we were greatly blessed with many old girls in all three groups, and many very wise and hard-working men as well.

When the missionaries started the first schools at the beginning of the century, it was a fairly simple matter to get there; fees were nominal, uniform basic, places exceeded demand and requirements were not high - just a willingness to learn.

As time went on everything changed except the hunger for learning. The demand for places in established schools far outstrips their capacity; the standard of entry goes up annually and fees have risen astronomically. The government's hopes of providing free education at any level have been dashed by the rising inflation, which in turn has been aggravated by endless civil wars. So instead of little barefooted children running along country lanes to a thatch-roofed single-unit schoolroom, you find children of three years old being driven to nursery schools, wearing uniform and taking lunch in plastic boxes ready to stay all day because their parents both work in order to raise about £100 for the privilege. By the age of ten, they are going to school at weekends also to receive drilling in the papers for the Primary Leaving Examination they will sit at twelve or thirteen. Unless they score eighty per cent in all four papers they may not get a place at one of the coveted boarding schools; and each year the number scoring that mark increases so soon it may be ninety per cent that is required, and since there must be an element of luck in the questions asked, it is obvious that some of the very best get left out. It is a big temptation to cheat or bribe or cause your child to repeat classes several times over, and such things will happen until there are more good schools.

The number of good schools is increasing, but this degree of competition favours the well-to-do, who have books and videos at home and who have been well educated themselves. It is hard for the child of a peasant farmer to break into the system, and no provision has yet been made for the non-academic, as even technical schools recruit their pupils from the leaving exam, and can now pick very good candidates as far as paper qualifications are concerned, though they may be all thumbs when they get to carpentry.

A few primary schools in rural settings have been able to combine basic education with some practical farming, and ideally agriculture, home economics and science are part of every upper primary syllabus; but the demands of the examination at the end soon lead both teachers and students to concentrate on English and maths. Ideally the first few years of school should be taught in the vernacular language, but Uganda has ten major languages, and once there is a mixture of tribes there is more than one language. This is especially the case in the towns, so English becomes the language of instruction even in nursery school; and for fear of getting behind in English the country schools soon follow their example. In the latest curriculum reform proposals this problem is redressed in theory, through a requirement that all students should take an African language at O level, but the major hurdle comes at the end of primary seven, and unless there is an African language there children won't be taught it. Kenya has no problem here. All children learn Swahili, but Uganda has never adopted Swahili or any of its own languages as the national one, and it is hard to see how there will ever be agreement as to which one it should be.

Getting on for 200,000 children sit PLE in November, and only about a quarter of them find secondary places. Those that do, join their schools about March and begin a very interesting course in fourteen subjects, and at boarding school anyway are exposed to libraries, physical education, housework and farming as well as formal science, French and all the usual academic subjects. Two years later they tend to be streamed and make choices of their O level subjects, nine or ten, which are supposed to include at least some sciences and a practical subject. The slogan is to produce "Job makers, not job takers," but it must be admitted that O level art or home economics or woodwork would be hard to sell as a skill.

Schools do their best to make this stage of education as meaningful as possible. Sport is encouraged, so are music and drama and debating, but many schoolteachers find it hard to give spare time to these activities as they are busy trying to supplement their meagre salaries by growing their food or taking another job. Parents help, and pay morale boosts three times the size of the basic salary, but it is never enough. This forces the students to become self-reliant and to initiate their own spare time activities until the pressure of the next exam comes along and they cannot be prised away from their books even at night!

After O levels, taken in November, students formally leave

school and go home for six months while the sixth formers take the A levels in March and the headteachers meet to select the two thousand or so who will return to school for the two-year A level course. The majority of schools have three streams at O level of about fifty students in each, and can only take back sixty for A level. A school where only a handful of their own students have qualified now receives a good input from better schools, while the best schools, where all may qualify, have to find places for about seventy-five students elsewhere. Many heads would understandably prefer to take back their own students, so it makes for some difficulties. These duly arrive in May and within a few months they have to take over the leadership of the school as the sixth year are getting near their finals. These are also very important since university places are few, and to qualify for medicine or law or commerce you need very good grades. There are no interviews: everything depends on the examination results.

There was a time at Gayaza when we had some Asian teachers, some of whom were very good, and when circumstances forced them to leave one of them said:

"Teaching at Gayaza is not so much a job as a way of life."

When I first joined the staff in 1957, I was the junior among twelve missionaries, and they were a formidable set. One had to be very careful indeed to maintain the high standards that had been built up over the previous fifty-two years since the school was started in 1905 to educate the daughters of chiefs to become suitable wives. When I found photographs in later years of the display at the school's Jubilee in 1955, I was astonished at the meticulous needlework and printing that was evident. When we celebrated our seventy-fifth and eightieth birthdays we had hardly anything to display of that quality; but the Old Girls still reveal what they were taught when they entertain or organise displays and it is good to know that such standards have only been eroded not eliminated.

By the late seventies the school had become a very different place in many ways. There were no tools for excellence. Books, paper, paint, none was available in quantity. They were either not there or were obtainable only at an exorbitant price. Numbers in classes had doubled; beds had all become double-deckers; meals had to be taken in shifts and because even plates and cutlery were in short supply the elaborate washing up procedures we followed in the sixties gave way to students bringing their own equipment and washing it up outside the dormitory. Instead of twenty fairly senior and experienced European staff we found ourselves with fifteen local recruits, still learning the job, and the young men seemed to have no control over teenage girls, and I often had to patrol the classroom area during lessons in case one got out of control. That has changed again now that Ugandans have taken over and many have had some years of experience; and the desire for education is so strong that very few students misbehave.

But this way of life the teachers referred to. What was it? It was partly a matter of standards. Anyone who taught at the school knew that they had a tradition of excellence to maintain, and for this reason it was hard to get staff for a long time, until we had enough Ugandans to encourage them (for we in turn became formidable!). As time went on and we went through the traumas of war many barricades came down as we had to solve the school's and the families' problems collectively. It was when we got to the level of sharing our last bottle of water or piece of soap that it began to occur to our colleagues that we "Bazungu" (white people) were their friends not their bosses. Gradually a sense of community grew stronger and stronger. It was helped by the necessity to do things for ourselves that we used to go out for, like church services, singing groups and then weddings and baptisms. Slowly we became Aunty to most of the staff children, and quite often godmother too, and one of us was called to be a go-between in a marriage problem when the parents were unwilling to let their daughter go. We were able to share the private lives of our fellow teachers very deeply, and while they probably think we did a lot of giving and they a lot of receiving the truth is that we were enriched beyond measure and so was the whole school community. And it all happened because Amin and Obote and their henchmen threw us together and into the presence of the Lord when we had nowhere else to turn.

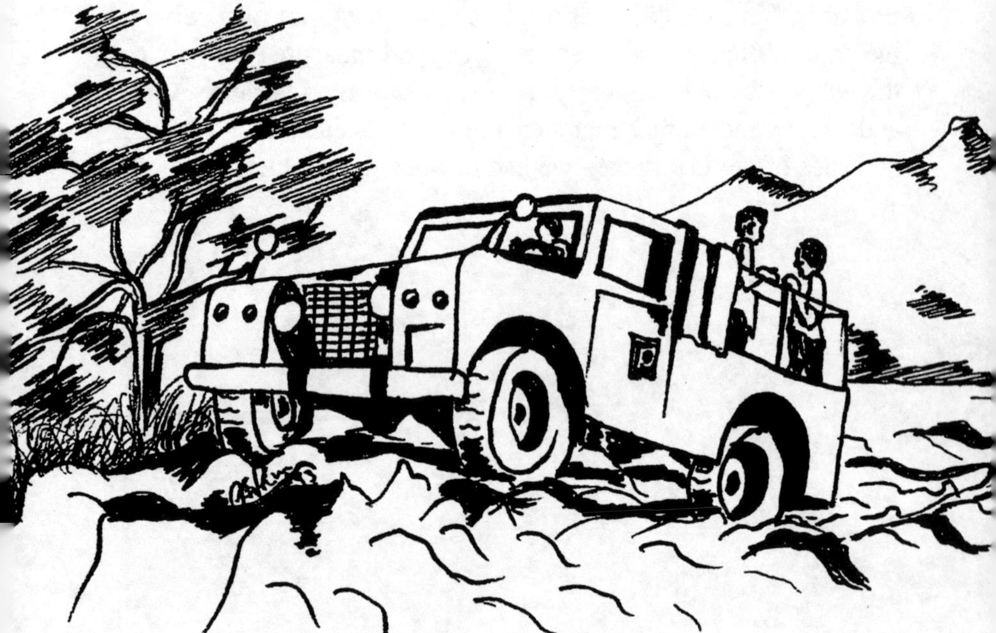

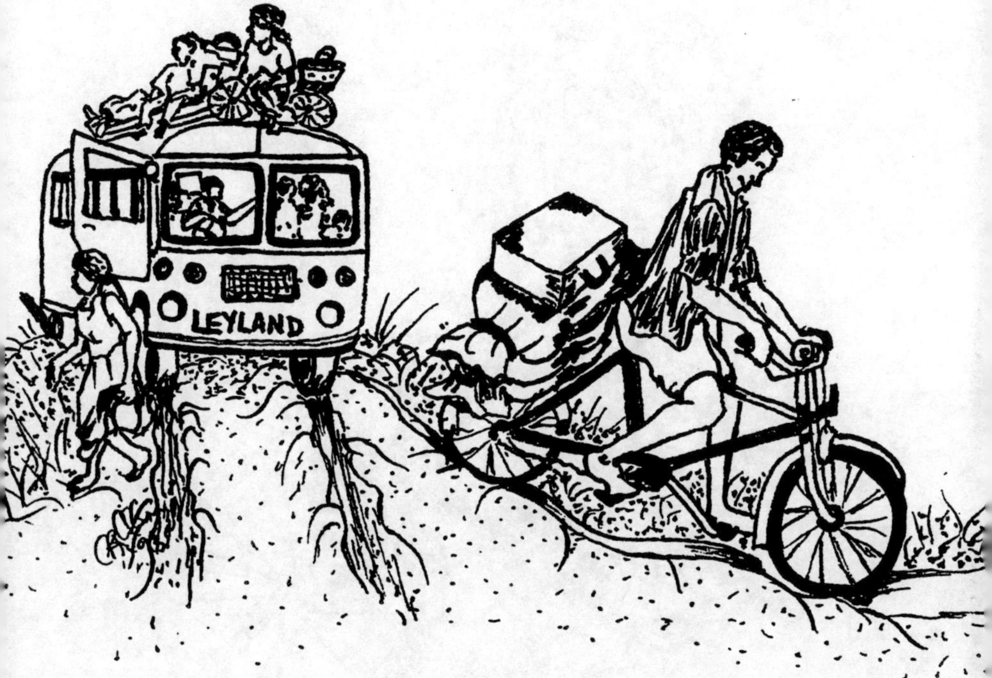
LEYLAND

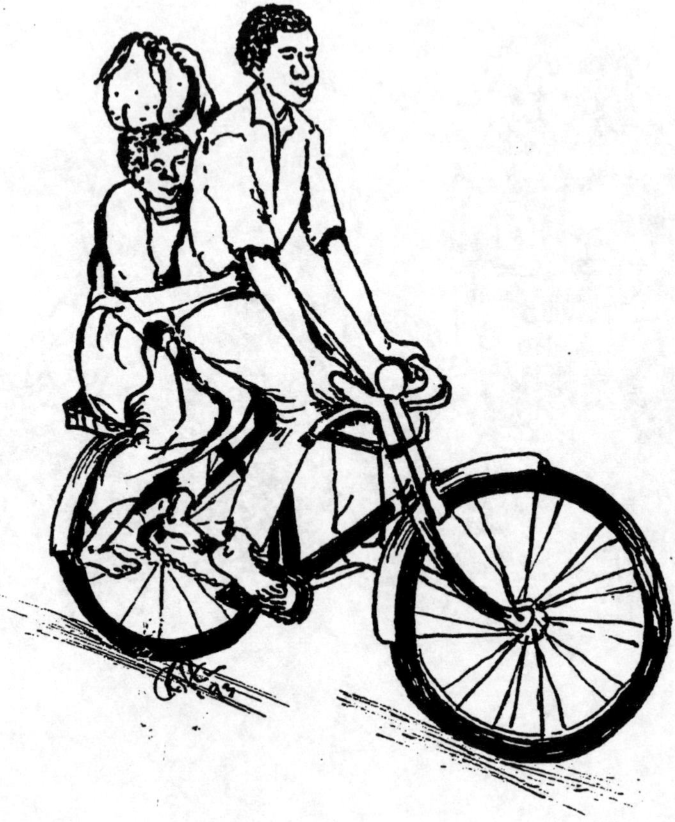

3. GOING OUT AND COMING IN

Means of transport, or as Ugandans usually refer to it, just 'means', figures large in Uganda, mainly as a problem. One trunk road goes from the Kenya border to Rwanda, from East to West, and in good times the main towns are linked by tarmac roads. Otherwise it is murram, which means clouds of dust in the dry season and mud, puddles and potholes in the rainy seasons, the worst time of all being just after heavy rain when the mud becomes sticky.

'Means' varies from the bicycle to the Mercedes Benz of the Ministers and business men. Taxis have increasingly become what the Kenyans call "matatu" - minibuses built for ten to twelve passengers which invariably carry twenty. Long distance buses exist, but often break down mid-journey or get stuck in the mud. Lorries carry passengers perched on top of the loads, and for many years few private cars could survive journeys outside Kampala, for spares were hard to come by and fuel was available only spasmodically and at an ever increasing price. There is no animal transport.

For the peasant farmer and the local employee a bicycle is a 'must'. He will use it as a means of getting himself and a great deal besides to his place of work or to the market. The carrier can take another person, two or three jerrycans of local beer, two whole branches of bananas, four or five cartons full of buns or loaves of bread, three sacks of charcoal or a whole load of banana leaves for wrapping meat. These will be carted ten or twelve miles and sold for some measure of profit. Traditionally, women do not ride bicycles, but they do sit sideways on the carrier, with a baby tied on behind, and baskets of shopping held in front. And many a famous present-day Ugandan remembers being taken to school in the carrier of Daddy's bike.

Lorries are ubiquitous and usually open-topped, with metal or wooden sides. Few are restricted to their official purpose such as delivering potatoes or bales of cloth. There will be passengers on top of the load, personal shopping or bartering material behind it; and when the goods are delivered it will become a temporary taxi or removal van. Boarding schools usually own lorries as they have to collect their own food and firewood, and often the smartly dressed students, off to a debate or a match, have to wait while the mud or sticks from the previous journey are cleared; and at the end of term the lorry becomes a taxi to the station, piled high with cases and mattresses.

Official journeys up-country are mainly by bus and often there is as much on top of the bus as inside it - suitcases and cardboard boxes, mattresses, bunches of bananas, even baskets full of live chickens. Fortunately, there are not many bridges over the road, but on one sad occasion when we took our girls to the coast we crossed the old pontoon bridge at Mombasa at high tide, and a harsh grating noise halfway across told us that not only cases but the metal edge of the luggage rack itself had been ripped by the overhead supports. It was a new bus, too.

Lorries are often the main means of travel to weddings and funerals. Ugandans are adept at covering their best clothes with old ones for the journey, and when a lorry whose capacity for passengers is fifty goes to a funeral it will probably squeeze in a hundred. It's not easy for the owner to refuse because the burial ground is sure to be well off the main road, and everyone has to be at the funeral.

The well-to-do have cars, of course. A long line of identical black Mercedes sits behind the International Conference Centre and purrs into life on public occasions. They belong to Ministers, who cannot afford to use them personally. Most people drive Peugeots and Datsuns, tough cars that can survive the appalling road conditions, and when there is petrol the fortunate go by car to the office, to school, to church and to market. The rest go by taxi or 'foot' it, and even quite small children walk seven or eight miles to school.

Running a school was very greatly dependent on transport, and whether it was the post-runner's bicycle - which was always in need of spokes and tubes, the HM's car - which was no better for having been borrowed by the army during a coup, the tractor - which did a sterling job for over ten years but cost us millions of shillings in repairs, the bus - which the lorry driver hated, or the lorry itself: each day would bring a transport problem of one kind or another. The vehicles broke down; parts were stolen; drivers went sick on important occasions; fuel was short; spares were unobtainable; or we would have promised to lend our vehicle to a neighbour, only to get a message to say that, 'Today without fail' we must go and collect some essential commodity from thirty miles away.

Perhaps you think that buying a bus is a simple matter, if you have the money, but in Uganda in the mid-seventies it was not simple at all. Ours was to be a Saviem, to replace the good old Leyland, which had been bought in the sixties when things were so much easier. The Leyland had gone down to Nairobi for an overhaul, but it returned in a worse state, if anything, and a new one was imperative.

First of all, I called at the French firm's premises and was told to collect the vehicle from The Ministry of Education. On arrival there I was directed upstairs to collect papers, and as I left to go down to take possession, someone shouted:

"Be sure you have the jack and all the tools as listed."

The warning was timely. As I rounded the corner, I saw the tools being quietly removed. To the driver's dismay, I stopped that operation and made a thorough search for any other possible losses. I was then informed that before it could be licensed it must be fitted with a fire extinguisher. One wondered why such an essential item was not provided! So Monday ended and Tuesday was spent scouring the town for a second-hand extinguisher, and I was warned that a second-hand one might not pass the inspector of vehicles. It was a risk we had to take.

Next I remembered that all such vehicles had to be fitted with reflectors. If you did not live in Uganda you might have expected that these too would be fitted before the bus was sold! Our next journey was five miles out of town to the factory which made all kinds of metal plates; but we got there to discover that on Wednesdays they sold beds: the day for reflectors was Thursday. So we went home without the bus once more, and every night it stayed in town it was prey to some kind of looting.

On Thursday we got the reflectors, but they couldn't fit them at the factory. We had to hire garage number plates and drive round in search of a garage big enough to accommodate a bus and small enough to be interested in such a simple task. Surely now the end was in sight! I drove fairly confidently back on Friday. All I had to do was to show the brand new bus, all kitted out with the accessories at the licensing office and go home for lunch. But once again I was to be disappointed. I was told the vehicle was subject to income tax, because it could be hired out for profit. We had no intention of letting it out of our sight, since it would carry food and firewood as well as passengers, and never be free. But who was going to believe me? No-one was very helpful, and I knocked somewhat nervously on the door labelled Mr Mukasa, Income Tax Inspector. To my surprise it was a lady's voice calling "Come in!" and to my delight there sat an old girl, whom I had taught some years back. There was no problem over tax; the only remaining difficulty concerned the shape of the number plates, but that was solved by a lucky chance, and late in the afternoon the bus drove proudly into the school. No-one rushed to meet it. One was overheard to say, "I suppose that's the new bus. I liked the red one better."

On its second day out with the new driver it had a minor accident and lost a lot of paint, and during the 1979 war it was nearly taken at gunpoint. The lorry driver would not have been sorry to say goodbye to it for it always let us down when we were far from home. On one occasion it "died" full of a ton of ground-nuts and had to be towed home by the old bus; another time it came to a halt outside the theological college, and the girls on board had to spend the night there with us having no idea where they were. In the end we decided to sell it and buy a lorry instead, as by then the girls were quite happy to board a lorry for outings. We sold it for seven million shillings, in cash, on a Friday afternoon, and I had to keep the money over the weekend till it could be banked! Seven million wasn't much in real terms, but it took up a lot of space in five and ten shilling notes! I never saw the bus again after we sold it, but I always felt it was a doubtful treasure.

For ten years the main road to Kampala was left unrepaired and the twenty-minute journey soon took forty. There came a time when the road up to the school itself was so rutted and so slippery that I hardly dared go on it alone, and wondered what would happen if we had a medical emergency when the driver was not there. Then suddenly the grader arrived in the trading centre, and when we jokingly remarked that he ought to come up to the school since we had a Minister in residence, he did just that.

Meanwhile some of the roads in Kampala had been graded and tarmacked. One was nicknamed London Road, and another was said to be as smooth as a baby's skin; the only trouble was that people began speeding to celebrate the end of the years of driving round potholes.

I have described how we bought a bus, though it never served us well. The first lorry we had was just after the 1979 war. We heard that some lorries which had been parked on the open-air cinema ground and had been looted were now back on site and could be had for a somewhat reduced price. They were Benz lorries and just right, except that we had quickly to paint over the name of the looter in case he tried to get it back, and there was no handbrake, no spare wheel and no right-hand driving mirror. These did not become available for years, and it meant going to the testing place annually and persuading the police that they should nevertheless pass the vehicle as roadworthy. When things seemed to improve, in the late eighties, we proudly ordered the missing pieces from Germany, but they were purloined. We finally got a new lorry when we had the good fortune to have three of the four necessary signatories to our request amongst the school's officials. It was not the end of our troubles, because one night someone removed the king-pin keeping the back wheels on, two yards away from the nightwatchman. Our chief comfort on that occasion was that they did the same to a government vehicle parked nearby; but this was the problem in Uganda: every time you caught up with yourself financially and thought,

"Now we can afford that project that has been waiting for so long,"

a theft would occur and you would be faced with a bill of a million shillings.

Yet God always provided for our needs. His provision of a tractor at the start of the 1979 War was the most memorable. We had ordered it, together with a plough and other farm tools, and at the moment when it became available for collection our driver left us. One or two of us had tractors included on our driving licences, but it would have excited far too much notice if a well-known white woman drove a tractor along the main road for twelve miles, quite apart from the lack of experience. Then, because the invaders reached Masaka, and it was largely destroyed, refugees ran back to Kampala, among them a local lad who had a licence and had been working for the Ministry of Agriculture.

He went to Kampala, escorted, and as darkness fell one March evening the tractor chugged down the drive. After that it never ploughed a field - the plough and other parts were lost in Kampala. It went out many times a day to fetch water, firewood and food. Tractors were the only means of transport not in danger of being stopped or looted, by order of Amin. As time went on the tractor wore out - its drivers all proved unreliable in one way or another. One of them decided to use it for his own private trading and was hijacked by the army, along with several farm hands who were there with him. A furious army captain stormed into the school and accused us of harbouring guerrillas. He was so angry that he stalked out of the office leaving his walkie-talkie behind and had to come back for it. We had drawn breath by then and were able to persuade him that the man was a rascal, certainly, but not a guerrilla. During the next few days we had to drive to the barracks and rescue the man and then the tractor along roads which had been deserted for months and where only army vehicles normally went. As usual, the Lord was with us and sent such a rain-storm when we were on our unescorted journey home that anyone considering ambush was bound to have taken shelter. What was even more amazing was that the storm stopped before the tractor reached that point and the car driver perched on the tractor was completely dry!

When it had cost us millions, we obtained a new one remarkably cheap. This time an Old Girl was able to help us cut out ten or twelve stages of red tape, and to our amazement and delight the farm manager came back with it the day after we had been to select it.

It was wonderful to own a car, but you needed strong nerves to drive it on bad roads, and most roads were bad most of the time. On holiday I remember best getting back into a car right in the middle of a game park, which stretched for a hundred miles in every direction, to find it would not start; but we had not sat for more than ten minutes when a Ford lorry passed by, and as ours was a Ford too he was able to show us how to dive down inside the bonnet and press a magic button and lo, it purred into life. The next time it stalled we were at an angle of thirty degrees up on a rock in the Olduvai Gorge, and it was a little more tricky - but it worked. And on the way home when we had to go through endless road-blocks it was actually a help because we explained what we were doing and intrigued the soldiers so much that they forgot to search the car for weapons. I once drove about six miles straddling a gully three feet deep, just waiting for the moment when it joined a ditch and I would have to reverse the miles again - but it did gradually even up and we were able to keep going. The next hazard was elephants, which could appear from round the corner and demand their right of way. Once, we had stopped for a cup of tea, and had just spread it all out on the bonnet when a whole family of elephants crossed the road just behind us. Not knowing what to do, we stood still, and the occupants of the cars which had to wait leant out and accused us of picnicking with the elephants. It had certainly not been our intention: elephants are very dangerous animals. Looking back from the viewpoint of the dangers from human enemies that threatened us in later years, I would not do those journeys again; but for his own reasons God looked after us and the courage we had had to practise then probably helped us to face the traumas of the war years.

Cars took the place of telephones most of the time I was in charge of a school in Uganda. Our line was out of use for over ten years, and on the few occasions when it was repaired, within a few days somebody stole the wires for washing lines or resale. In emergencies it was no joke to have to leap into the car and dash to hospital or the police or in search of a home miles away; but there was no alternative, and it did give us some respite from interruptions and importunate callers. They also had to make a journey. The annoying thing was that when you reached the city, telephones did work and your interview with officials could take ages because the phone kept interrupting. At times I used to ring from the reception area and let it be thought that I was ringing from the country: that way you saved a lot of time and your interview could not be terminated till you put down the receiver.

When I first took over the school, the phone worked but it could take an hour to connect and when it did it was necessary to bellow to be heard, so nothing confidential could be discussed: everyone within twenty yards of the office could hear.

We still had the phone when President Amin's daughter was in the school, and each time I had to communicate with State House, I feared for my job if I said the wrong thing. His last call was when he was on the run, and he rang to ask for his children to be ready in twenty minutes.

Exactly twenty minutes later a small car with its windows totally blacked out with mud collected the two girls and we never saw them again. That week girls were fetched in hijacked buses and ambulances, in cars, on bicycles and even wheelbarrows, and in a lorry with no back at all. When the war ended they all returned safely, including one who had gone as far as Saudi Arabia in a dhow. During the hostilities one parent, who was a Minister, came on an old bicycle to check on his daughters, with the news that the army were just passing the bottom of his garden, and was surprised to find her ringing a bell for prep. School went on through everything: it was important to keep ourselves occupied, and not have time to imagine what might happen to us any minute. Thanks to the tractor, we were able to collect water and food, and thanks to being off the main road the soldiers went past, not through, our compound. The only tank that ventured along our main road was blown up six miles from us, and at that time most visitors came on foot, having concealed their vehicles, if they had any, from the many potential hijackers. The school car was taken once, in my absence, but I managed to persuade the army commander to return it when term started. The repairs cost a quarter of a million shillings and it was never paid because a new government came to power who disclaimed responsibility for the damage. But we counted ourselves lucky to get it back at all, and did not fuss overmuch. The windscreen had been damaged earlier, and remained cracked for years. I promised the police I would replace it when the roads were repaired, little thinking that would be five years later.

Gradually the roads were mended, and new vehicles appeared on the roads as the number of potholes decreased; but sadly, the old toll of road accidents came back, and many were killed through collisions with unlit lorries, or as a result of overcrowded taxis, let alone speeding along the new tarmac. Even the goats and chickens had to learn that roads were dangerous again.

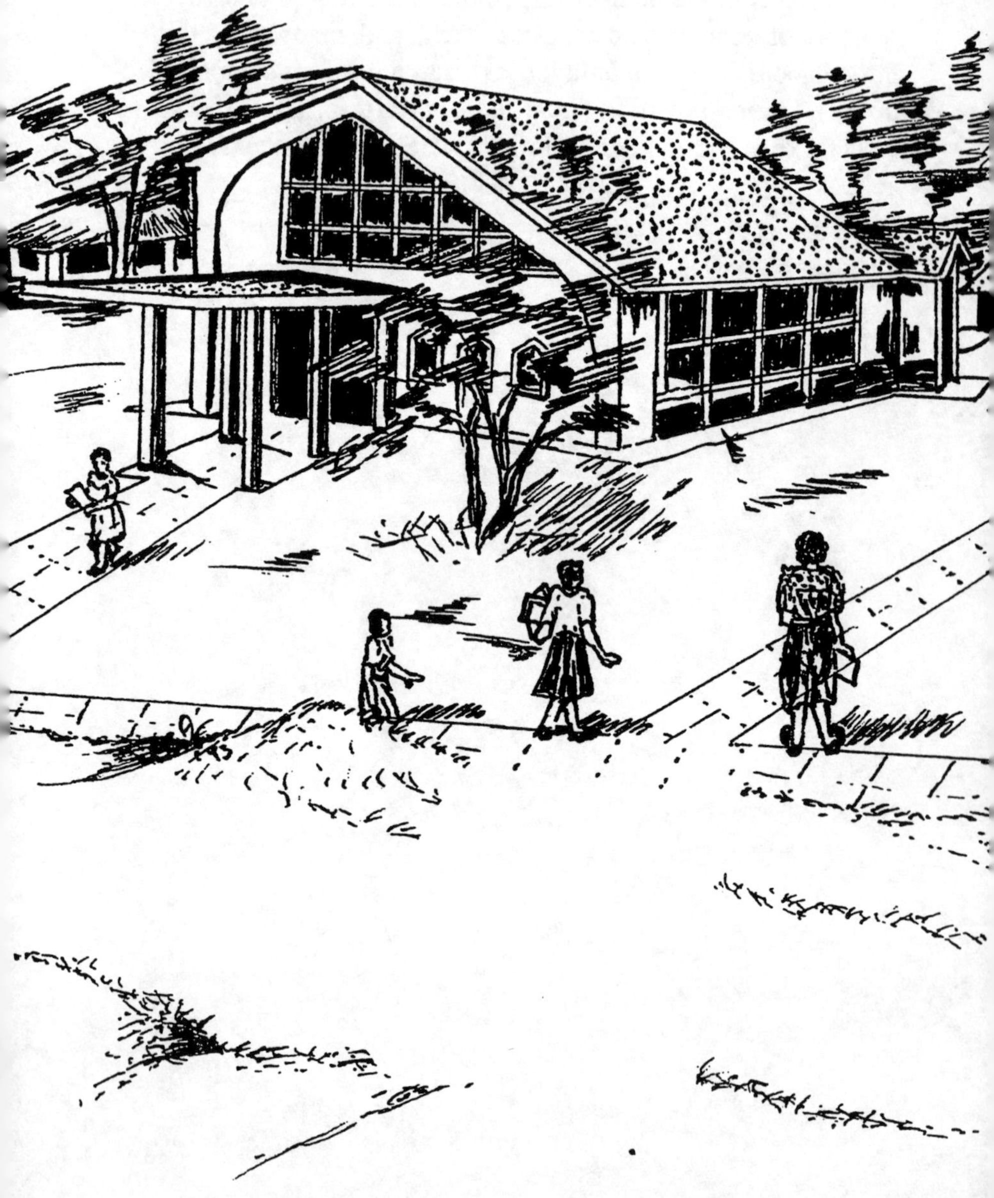

4. NEVER GIVE UP

Being a boarding school meant that we had to organise the day from six am till bedtime. From the very beginning in 1905 the parents' anxiety that the girls should not forget how to dig was respected, and at six thirty each morning the whole school is engaged in farming, housework or PE till breakfast, which is no feast - just a cup of sweet tea or a bowl of liquid porridge or a handful of popcorn. By eight am all are in uniform and on their way to class time or assembly. This happens in two shifts as the school chapel, which has to double as an assembly hall, cannot hold more than two-thirds of the school. A hymn, a reading and a prayer followed by notices, first for the seniors and then the juniors, begins the day. On Wednesdays, the juniors stay in the classrooms and have their own prayers there, led by one or two of them, since not all staff are Christians, while the seniors have the full twenty minutes in the chapel - prayers followed by a talk or demonstration or reading of something thought provoking. Sometimes the prefects will act a role play about table manners or how to wear uniform, and repeat it next day for the junior assembly. However hard-hitting the topic may be, it will be greeted with applause. Drama is very dear to Ugandans, and during the repressive regimes a great deal of political criticism of the government delighted audiences in the National Theatre, usually unchecked by the authorities, and more and more local theatres are springing up near markets and in the villages, always well attended, even if there are no seats. This is why drama is such a powerful medium for evangelism in schools, and it was exploited to the full at Gayaza - not in a compulsory assembly but at voluntary services, which would be crowded to the doors.

Six lessons took place in the morning, most of them double periods for the senior classes, and as the labs were a good three minutes' walk from the classrooms, about two hundred girls were on the move up and down the compound in between. The staff would meet for coffee mid-morning, and some of the girls had "grub" in the dormitory to sustain them till lunchtime. Lunch was the big meal of the day: the girls ate in two shifts, taking their own plates and cutlery and washing them up in the dormitory afterwards. The menu would be one course - potatoes and beans, maizemeal and peas, cassava and beans or on high days plantain and a small piece of meat. There was hardly ever a pudding, so the girls bought their own bananas and bread or cakes as supplements. These were sold in the school canteen, which was run in later years by the teachers as a way of making a little extra money. In most cases the students had more to spend on extra food than the teachers earned in a full month's salary!

Rest hour was sacrosanct at Gayaza. Everyone had been up since six am and few would be in bed by ten pm so nothing was allowed to interrupt the chance to lie flat or study quietly from 1.30 to 2.15. Two lessons took place before tea - just a quick cup - and the four half-hour periods filled the remaining daylight hours with games, dancing, music practice and clubs. On Fridays the sixth formers would go visiting the old ladies in the nearby homesteads, chatting to them, doing their shopping and, if they were poor, taking along a small bag of sugar or salt. They often returned with sticks of sugar cane or even eggs in exchange. The very poor are in Uganda, as everywhere, the most generous of all.

Supper, again in two shifts, was served as darkness fell, because the dining room staff did not all live on the compound, and at seven thirty the drum would go for optional evening prayers in the chapel, led by the teachers four days a week, and once by the girls. I used to attend whenever possible, and heard many a powerful sermon from a teenager that would have impressed a professional. At the end of prayers the few teachers present would remain behind and pray for one class each night, by name. This was a tradition going back many years, and has never been dropped.

Then came prep for everyone, longer for senior classes, and as the juniors were released they would go home shouting to scare the ghosts: many were quite afraid of the dark. We had so much petty thieving from the dormitories that one class stayed behind each night on guard. Even so, blankets would be polefished through a window, and some thieves had the nerve to walk into a room and take suitcases full of clothes. It was all because of the extreme poverty around us. So many people had had their only blanket looted that you could understand why it seemed to them that a roomful of covered beds meant wealth untold.

The girls slept in seven dormitories, five of which had A level wings, so were easy for the prefects to supervise. The other two were the largest and the most difficult to control. Two house leaders were responsible to the prefects for what happened but the older girls came down later from prep, so there could be a lot to see to when they did arrive.

Saturday was washing day. Every girl had to wash her sheets, uniform and personal things during the day. They would be spread out on the grass, hung on lines or hung from window handles and trees. The junior classes had no organised prep on Saturdays so they really enjoyed free time at the shop and on the games courts without being edged aside by bigger girls. As soon as prep was over all the courts would be full all day long, left regretfully when meals or a roll-call called them away. Tennis on four handmade hard courts, badminton, volleyball and teniquoit on the only piece of flat ground the school had, which happened to be all round the chapel, and table tennis in our homemade recreation room, kept many happy for hours. The senior classrooms and the library would be full of the studious seniors, who seemed to have an insatiable thirst for reading. After tea on Saturdays there was often a class or house concert, with a play, dances and songs in English and vernacular languages. Not very much outside entertainment could be found, but in 1989 we were given a video and TV by a school in England, so that could also be watched. We paid a little to go in, to save for repairs and materials for it. Occasionally another school would bring a play, such as a set book for O or A level, and we did produce our own more serious drama too.

The highlight of Saturdays for the sixth form girls was that every three weeks they had a day out, when they could go home or visit the city freely till dusk, and about once a term they would be invited to a social at a boys' school, which would lead to about two thirds of them setting off by bus or lorry, to the huge excitement of the middle school, who would gather in hordes to cheer them on their way and greet them on return as if they had been in battle. They got so wild with excitement that the prefects had to police the occasion quite fiercely, sometimes even confining them in the classrooms till the returnees were all back in the dormitories! For this reason we did not return the invitation.

Clubs also went out now and then, to debate or attend a seminar. A club which had no prospect of a visit to another school had little chance of good membership. The Wild Life Club was extremely popular, probably because there was the remote chance of visiting a game park one day.

The Christian Club was one of the most popular and catered for the whole school. Sundays would begin with the few Roman Catholics going out to Mass, while breakfast was a little later than on weekdays. At 9.20, the O level musicians would beat the four drums in their varied rhythms to call the school to the Sunday Service. All had to attend the roll call, but the service was optional. Between three and four hundred would stay, especially if the service was Holy Communion, and the chapel choir would lead the singing with great fervour. Sometimes the preacher was from outside, though seldom Anglican clergy; sometimes the speaker would be one of us, and we always led the service, to keep it lively and vaguely liturgical. During their final term, the school leavers would take an entire service, involving all those who normally attended the year Bible study, which could be fifty of them. Some led prayers, some read, one would give a testimony and one would preach. It gradually became a tradition for them to compose and sing a new song or two, and some of these are in the school hymn book and on the Gayaza Praise tapes, so have reached a far wider audience than they expected.

After service, the school was free for the day, and many went to read in the classrooms: they had nowhere else to sit, apart from their beds. The staff at the service would always meet for coffee, together with any visitors, such as those from the university community next door. Small babies in their best clothes would be admired, and the news of the week would be shared before we went off to cook lunch and have a rest. The Christian Club happened after tea, when over two hundred girls and several staff would meet, sing informal songs in English and vernacular languages, listen to serious talks, watch mimes and plays and share testimonies. Christians on the staff would be invited to share in turn, and if a member of staff became a Christian, he or she would immediately be invited to come and say so and there would be great rejoicing. It was often humbling to listen to the girls' testimonies, as they shared the opposition and persecution they met at home, the burdens they carried in broken homes, the threat of witchcraft and its practices, and some of the costly reconciliations that took place within the very close school community. Their openness often put us to shame.

From time to time, some seniors of the club with the more musical staff would meet after supper and learn some of their recently composed songs and make a programme that could be shared around Kampala in schools, colleges and churches. As soon as that session was finished, the drum would call the rest of the members and they would sing till bedtime. They were indefatigable!

All day Saturday and Sunday, parents and friends were allowed to visit, and for many this was the high spot of the week. Problems could be shared, and 'grub', in the form of bananas, pineapples, biscuits, nuts and popcorn, would be carried down to the dormitory larder. The fear of starvation would recede, and some would share with their less visited friends. Parents became a very important part of the school, because government fees and grants could not possibly meet all the requirements, and parents had to be asked to supplement them with money for food, transport, medicine, building, and teachers' salaries, thus multiplying the official fees several times over. They were happy to do it if they knew the PTA Committee had agreed, and as time went on they did even more by fund-raising, taking up issues with officialdom, and even organising and paying for the restoration and decoration of buildings that had not seen a coat of paint since the 1960's.

We had no say about who came to teach in the school, but we were immensely blessed as time went on to have representatives of every tribe joining the four older European teachers, and most years we had a young volunteer from England, filling in between school and college to remind the Ugandans that not all "Bazungu" were antique. The Ugandans were either trained graduates from Makerere University or diplomates from one of the post A level teachers' colleges. Quite often we had teachers on teaching practice and this gave both sides the chance to decide whether or not they would stay on afterwards. For many years we were desperately short of staff, and I remember several years when we were without a teacher for A level chemistry or economics; and yet the students passed. This was probably when the business of holiday coaching began, which became such a nightmare to the regular teachers later, when students would cut lessons, or sit and compare notes with what the professor had said during the holidays. University places were not easily obtained, especially in medicine, law and economics, so it was tempting to go for coaching just in case it helped you to that extra mark. But it was a system very demoralising to young teachers and we did our best to discourage it.

Running a school such as ours was a daily nightmare, although we were in many ways far better off than most schools. We had dormitories with tiled roofs, and permanent classrooms. We could house all our teachers, though some lived in a single room. We had an excellent school cateress, with long experience, who never produced a meal late, even when there was nothing but wood fires to cook on, and there was no vehicle to fetch firewood. We had a farm, which supplied milk to the staff families and even some for the schoolchildren. We had ninety acres of farmland, although many of the crops would be stolen at night. We had a lorry, which was not commandeered by the army, and a tractor and gangmower capable of keeping the grass cut. We had a fairly reliable work force who would put in two or three hours of work daily for the pathetic official wage we paid them. They were happy to belong to us and have an ID card as labourers, so avoiding being taxed on their coffee plantations at home. They also gained from the contents of aid parcels full of old clothes, which might well be Sunday best to them. We had a library, whose books were not looted or burnt by passing soldiers. We had games fields, even if the hockey pitch was nine feet higher one side than the other. We had four tennis courts, each one patiently covered and rolled by generations of players and punishments!

Above all, we had a wonderful staff, both teaching and non-teaching, who seldom gave up, no matter how adverse their living conditions were, and who worked very hard in school to keep up standards and out of school to maintain their own basic needs. All had to have some other source of income, and yet a teacher on duty had to be in school from eight am to ten pm.

Even so, it was like riding the back of a tiger to keep the school going, and the only thing that kept one sane was the fact that any crisis situation would very soon be overtaken by another. If we did not have a critical shortage of teachers, we had a shortage of housing for them. If the lorry was in working order for a Saturday outing, the driver would be off sick or at a funeral. If one took on a senior class who had no English teacher, one would suddenly be called to a day-long meeting in town and miss the lessons. If one chose Thursday for a day off, and looked forward to a pleasant break visiting friends in Kampala, Thursday would bring a medical emergency, and the day would be spent in hospital waiting rooms or searching for the child's parents. If one stayed in to get on with office work, a delegation would arrive wanting to see over the school. If one went out, one would return to find that someone very important had called, which would mean a trip back to town next day to see him. And for ten years the road to Kampala was all ruts and bumps, to say nothing of up to five road-blocks on the way.

Worst of all was the daily line of would-be parents, bringing every kind of letter and plea for a place for their precious daughter. All the officials knew the school was full, but they had to get their offices cleared, so they sent them on to the schools, where almost all had to be refused, but not before one had listened to all the reasons why this child was uniquely suited to the school. If the child came too, dressed in her best, it was all the harder to say NO. The other staff used to say I had a weakness for white socks, but that only meant the young ones: they looked so eager, and so deserving that one's heart bled for them. Every January we used to interview about fifty for four or five places, and once again refusing was intolerably painful, unless you had reason to suspect that the parents had tried to get a preview of the papers, which was not impossible.

A good many applicants had no right whatsoever to a place. They were using the influence of high officials to get in. These got very short shrift, but it all took hours of time, and if the office was closed they would follow you home and bang on the door there. I had a big house, so I would go out of earshot as fast as I could. There again one could miss the visit of a friend or old girl by pretending to be deaf.

Old Girls were the final reward of teaching for a number of

years in the same school. They went on to do such interesting things, and would sometimes return in a professional capacity at useful moments. Doctors would come to give free examinations, and a water engineer got our tank cleaned out over a week of public holidays one year, climbing into it herself to make sure the job was well done. Several found their way on to the Board of Governors, and when one who had just qualified as a doctor turned up for blood doning, the numbers doubled. One Minister cut out days and weeks of red tape for us when we needed a new tractor, and at the same time galvanised the Old Girls' Association into action. I remembered her energies at school being rather less usefully directed, but as a Minister she was efficient and highly respected by her male colleagues. Like so many, she did us credit.

We were not the only good school for girls, even though many used to call us The School. There was an equally good Roman Catholic school, and we both often topped the list in national examinations, to the mixed pride and chagrin of the Ministry. Generally speaking, despite the low position women had in Ugandan culture, merit was recognised, and women soon found their way into politics, the law, medicine and even engineering. Our first engineering student had to go and study in Nairobi, and was accepted on the assumption that she was a man. They tried to refuse to keep her, but at the end of the first year she came top, so naturally she was allowed to complete her degree. She was the first of many.

Women were quite soon admitted for ordination, but the majority made their greatest contribution as wives and mothers, and through the Mothers' Union, YMCA, Uganda Womens' Effort to Save the Orphans and similar organisations have given outstanding service to the nation's welfare and development.

NEVER GIVE UP

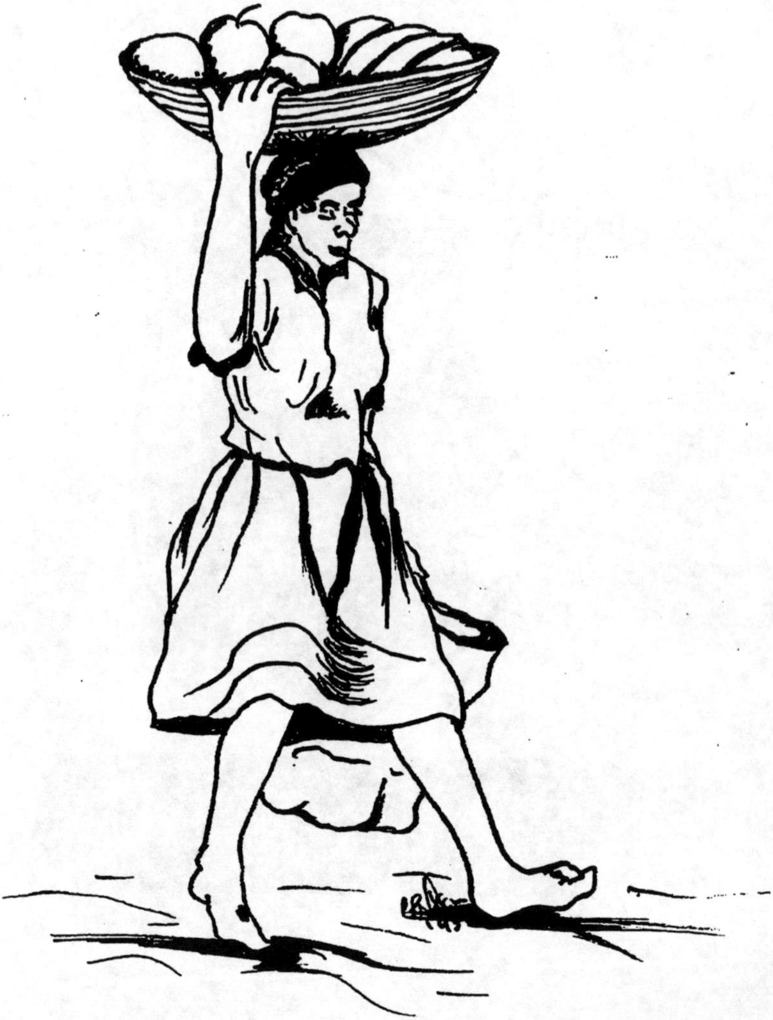

5. NOT MANY MIGHTY ARE CALLED

"Eeee! nyabo! Nga kitalo! Eeeeeee!" My house servant, Alice was kneeling on the ground before me in an agony of grief: "Madam, a terrible thing has happened."

For a moment I thought someone had died, but when I managed to calm her she finally blurted out that she had boiled the kettle dry and it was refusing to function. Her face when I pushed in the red button, which miraculously still worked after years of kettle abuse, was worth seeing.

"Kitalo! Amazing!"

Alice must have been in her forties when I took her over from my predecessor in the house. I remember her telling me that her sixteen-year-old daughter was getting married at about that time. She went on working till the day I left, washing, ironing, sweeping, dusting, washing-up - and on the rare occasions when she broke a cup or a glass, she would hang around till I came out of school and show me the broken bits. I was never angry, because she was so careful, but she would tremble as she confessed. Her zeal at washing was such that my towels were ragged with the wringing they received, and it was hard to convince her that some things didn't need ironing. She was no cook, but she could manage a panful of potatoes and the Saturday 'goo' - a mixture of eggplant, onion, tomato and curry which invariably graced our supper table on the one night I entertained friends, and occasionally she would bring maize or cassava from her plot as a thank-you for having had it ploughed, and add that to the menu. She earned about 2,000/- a month, till I discovered that she was being charged 1,000/- for the hovel she rented to live in. As I left, we set her on the way to start building a house for herself, but I wondered what had become of her children, who should have taken care of her. She sang tenor in the church choir, and never missed a service there. Service seemed to be what she was born to and she did it with all her might, asking very little of life in return.

Until she died in her eighties, old Susannah used to look in from the village quite frequently, sometimes accompanied by her brother who had documents to prove that he had fought with the British Army in the war. We would exchange such conversation as I could manage in her language for a while, but I knew the real purpose of the visit was that she had run out of sugar or soap. These were not only short in Uganda but desperately expensive. I would pretend that I had just happened to think of giving her a little, and she would pretend that she never dreamt of receiving a gift. At times she would bring a few eggs, but usually it was a pure scrounge. After her death, another brother, Besweri, a church teacher, lived in her house, and as he got too old to visit, we would go to him. He would sit regally in the arm-chair we had given him, which dated back to the early missionaries' time, and talk away. One table would be covered with a variety of medicines he had been prescribed - probably over several years - and another would have an embroidered cloth and a large Bible on it. Discreetly hiding his bed - for the house was just one room - would be a bright cloth of several yards length, hanging from a string. The chairs were home made, very low on the ground and folding, modelled on the old type of camp chair from the First World War. His memories were fascinating to listen to, and I was sorry not to have more time to go and hear them. The trouble was that the rules of hospitality required people to offer food and drink to all visitors, and he could not afford it, so one tended to go only when there was a death or some other reason for a brief courtesy call. I doubt if he will still be in this world when I go visiting Uganda again; but, if not, he will certainly be in heaven. There were so many rogues and villains around in Uganda that men like Besweri, and women like Alice stood out strongly for their innocence and integrity. They owned nothing, but they did not envy what others possessed.

Neither did Daudi, our nightwatchman. He came to Uganda as a refugee from Rwanda in about 1960, along with two others. One of them left when his son finished secondary school about ten years later, but the other two stayed on and say they will die there. Daniel is known as 'Flat Cap', because he always used to wear a cap on duty and no one could get their tongue round his long Rwandese name. He must have been a soldier, for whenever the HM's car drew up at the gate, he would stand at attention and salute before opening the gate, no matter how much amusement this caused. Every pay day he would get drunk, but even then he could find his hat and get his hand to it. Daudi, though just as old, was a different sort, gentle and generous to his employers, though he could bully his fellow watchmen if he saw the need. One day he came in great pain and needed an operation urgently. I saw him at the hospital about to be given a bed, and saw that he had a friend to look after him there, and we promised to pay his bill. To my horror, two hours later he was back at school, thirteen miles away. As soon as my back was turned someone had come in and bribed their way to his bed and he was simply told to go home! My fury knew no bounds, but the operation had to be done, so we sank our pride and went and begged a parent from the school to do it in his private clinic for a nominal fee, and Daudi's life was saved, though it was a long time before he was on the beat again.

He used to sell bananas and bread and toffees to supplement his income; but he would be up on my verandah almost every week with an offering of some kind from his shop, which he could ill afford. I suppose being with us gave him a measure of security. Whenever I passed him on the compound at night he would greet cheerily, and I tried to interest him in the stars. He would say, "God is wonderful!" but I don't think he noticed much! Every month he would bring all the torches for new batteries and help me fill them, muttering about the carelessness of those who had obviously left their torches on till the cells ran out. I used to threaten to fine them, but I knew they couldn't pay.

One night as I came up the compound, I heard a noise in the store, so I rushed back to call the men I had just greeted on my way. There was no-one there, but I shouted and soon they reappeared rather sheepishly and came reluctantly to see my "burglar" saying, "Musisi has come back". We had had a workman of that name, but I couldn't see what that had to do with it. We found nothing and I went on. Then the curtains in my bedroom blew out at right angles, and I realised that there was an earth tremor and this had caused the shaking of the shutters. Next day, Alice greeted me with great excitement:

"Musisi came back, Musisi came back!" At last I got there. Musisi is Luganda for earthquake!

Another character on our compound for many years, till he died of cancer, was Edward, who became headman of the work force. He was no leader, but he was quite a good builder, so he soon persuaded me to let him do some contract building. Alas, he had no idea what a contract was, and always came back for more money for materials and more time. Many thousands of shillings later I appointed another headman and gave him the job of builder, on salary. He had an endless supply of children, all needing school fees or jobs. One actually joined our school and passed her exams, and another was a very good lab attendant, till thugs murdered him in the village one night. When Edward himself died, we went along to the burial, and he was wrapped in barkcloth like any simple villager, despite all his skills. One day he really did expect to become rich. Amin had been defeated and people were looting all over the town, so Edward took his family and quietly looted the contents of the chief's house: carpets, typewriter, furniture, whatever they could carry. He walked quite openly through the village, smiling and waving as he went. Next day, complaints reached the school that "our" man was a thief. I called him and realised from his guileless replies that he thought war meant the right to loot. He solemnly took it all back and was never prosecuted; but he must have cost the school a great deal with his artless accounting and casual building programmes.

Being situated in a small country village area, we had to employ fairly unskilled people, and suffered a lot of inconvenience; but what they lacked in skill and speed they made up in loyalty, and many worked faithfully for years on end with little reward, beyond a little aid from parcels and a blind eye turned to their propensity for sneaking off early or drinking the major part of their wages. One pay day the watchmen left their shoes at the gate and arrived barefoot. They had heard that there was an issue of shoes for another group, so decided to try their luck. When one was summarily dismissed for drinking, he rolled up the drive shouting, "Bye-bye the High". It was funny and sad but it also showed the affection the local people had for their main source of employment.

The workmen had one thing in common with the students,

which was a capacity for coping with tragedy and trauma, and in the end it is those who carried on, no matter what befell them, that one remembers most vividly.

One such was Kezia, later to become a wife to Amin, and to suffer appallingly before she was murdered at his hands. She arrived at the school from the far north of the country, where her father was a clergyman. She was an astounding actress, and was still quite young when she was chosen to play Joseph in a big pageant to celebrate laying the foundation stone of the school chapel. The brothers put her in a real hole in the ground and her plight was so appealing that big men were in tears as they watched. It was a performance none of us was to forget. She belonged to the very first group to return for sixth form studies, and a special plane was laid on to bring her to school, since transport by road could have taken a week or more. When she left, she went to train as a teacher, and on the way met Amin. We saw her occasionally in her capacity as one of the First Ladies, but a few weeks before her death, she came and told me how desolate she was at the brutal murder of one of her cousins and how she was going to refuse to bear Amin's child. When that refusal cost her her life, my mind went back to Joseph, and the way she had identified with his suffering. Many years later, I was sorting out old letters that had been written to me when I was going through a time of impending bereavement, and I found at least five written by Kezia at that time, from school, keeping me in touch with what they were doing, and understanding how I felt waiting for a loved one to die. I wished I could have been by her side in her anguish; but for any European to show up near Amin was to make matters deadly dangerous for whoever one visited.

We quite often took on disabled children, provided they could get around the enormous compound somehow. The one downstairs classroom had to be reserved for that class, and several ramps were erected in the dormitories to enable them to propel their wheel chairs in and out. Fortunately these were all at ground level. One such was Deborah, who was not apparently disabled when she arrived, but was soon found to have bone cancer in her leg. She went into hospital for treatment at a time when a visit to Kenya for more specialised care was almost impossible, though we pressed hard for it. Eventually she came out of hospital, persuaded that she would have a better future taking science, with a view to becoming a lab assistant, than hoping to get around as a lawyer. So she began to read sciences, trusting that she would soon be back at school. Meanwhile, she became adept at touring the hospital in her chair, and seemed to be known in every ward.

There was a remission, and she returned to school; but only a few weeks later I was called urgently. She had collapsed in tears of pain and had to be rushed back to hospital. It was obvious that we should not see her back. When we arrived and had to ask for assistance to get her to bed, one orderly after another rushed to the scene. "Deborah! Our friend! You have come back to us!" But Deborah could do no more for them or anyone. At her funeral, we realised just how much her cheerful acceptance of her lot and her quiet faith in God meant to dozens of patients. At school she might have been a recipient of kindness, but in hospital she was a light shining in a dark place. For those were very dark times. She could probably have been helped to live much longer, but we could not get through the bureaucracy needed to arrange an operation abroad.

At one time I had to have an emergency operation myself, on the very day that Amin had threatened to expel all the Europeans. I was just on my feet again for the funeral of another man I can never forget, His name was Benoni, and he had been brought up in Sanyu Babies' Home. He did well in later life, and when I knew him he was a respected and deeply loved clergyman, father and grandfather. He had not been taught much English in his youth and spoke it haltingly, compared with his brilliant children. But we invited him to preach at school, because the love and truth of God were so vivid in his life. In those days girls at secondary school could be merciless to anyone making a mistake. Even in class, they would never let a slip go by without comment. Benoni was not likely to get through his sermon without some mistakes.

"I am an old man now," he began, "but Jesus is my refugee, my eternal refugee."

Not one face betrayed even a glimmer of a smile. He had them all eating out of his hand; and because of the error we all remembered what he had said. As I sat outside the cathedral on the day of his burial nearly ten years later, I could hear him still.

Many of the girls I taught did great things in life and reached posts of enormous importance and responsibility: everyone knows them. These quiet, simple people of the village will not have their stories told or remembered; but it is a fact that behind all the success of the gifted, and alongside the corrupt and the cruel who have done so much to destroy Uganda since Independence, are hundreds of men and women who have just got on with life as they found it, seeking nothing beyond the necessities of life, and often lacking them. They should not be overlooked when people wonder how so much that is good and true and lovely survived even the worst that our enemies could do.

For not many mighty are called... God chose the poor, rich in faith. (I Cor I.26)

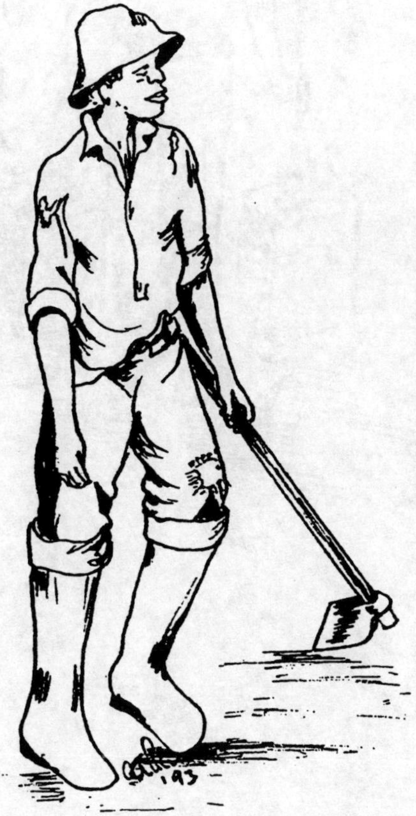

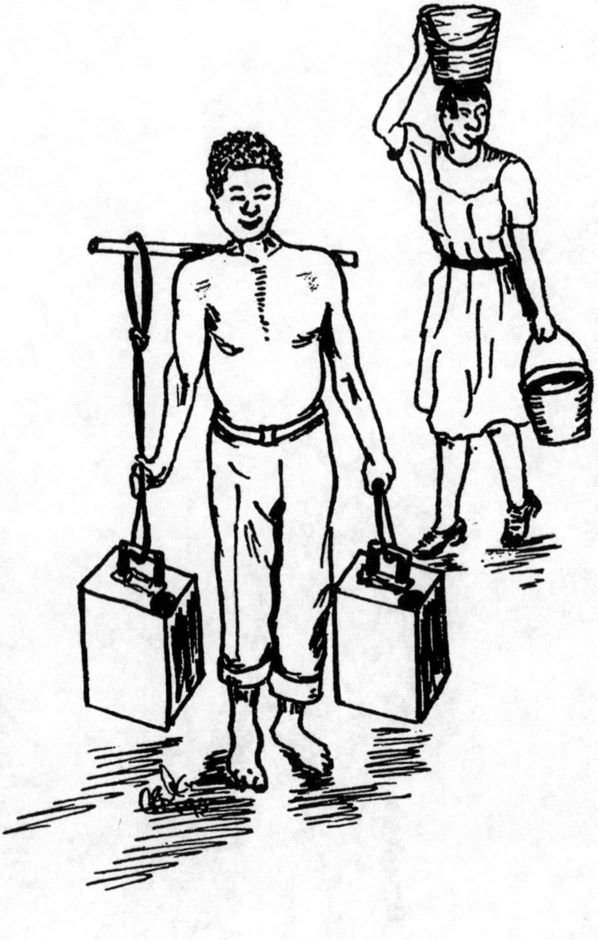

6. LOAVES AND FISHES

In the 1960's everything was available in Uganda for most people. Food was cheap. Roads were maintained, and more and more were tarmac. New buildings were going up all the time. Shops were full of materials and clothes from all over the world. One could buy a second-hand car for three hundred pounds and the AA was around to come to its rescue. Holidays at the coast or round the game parks were a possibility for any teacher, even those on mission salaries. It was all so apparently idyllic that when one went home on leave one's friends and relations would say:

"But you're not a proper missionary, having it all so good, with the sunshine thrown in as well!"

It was hard to justify one's existence then, but a few years later, the tone changed:

"How can you stay in Amin's country? Isn't your presence a kind of support to his policies?"

We could soon qualify for being "proper missionaries", if by that people meant that you had to cope with shortages. And as for its being Amin's place, we were at pains to insist that it was God's place, and we stayed to identify with all who meant it to be so again, and at their request. In the end it was clear that just by being there alongside, even when we had a way of escape denied to our colleagues, we did more than ever we achieved professionally.

In 1965, an old girl who was a prominent member of Government laid the foundation stone of one of the buildings given by USAID; and a year later we expected the Kabaka, who was President, to come and open it. Then, suddenly, we found we were getting no replies to our telephone inquiries or letters. And then the news broke that the palace had been surrounded and the Kabaka - the traditional king - had escaped through a gap in the wall and fled the country, never to return.

After the coup in 1971, Amin brought back his body for traditional royal burial. This was a clever diplomatic stroke, because it helped to win the majority tribe to his side. The atrocities of Obote's Regime, directed against this tribe, were another reason why Amin gained support; but his popularity began to wane when he expelled the Asians, threatened the Europeans, and plunged the country into an economic war which was still raging twenty years later. Then he too, resorted to thuggery, torture, and a new reign of terror. The ridiculous claims he made, and his bombastic style, led the world to see him as a buffoon, a sort of crazy bear, and it became hard to convince outsiders how dangerous he was. And glad as we were to be rid of him in 1979, things went from bad to worse for ordinary people, because guerrilla activity never stopped and any slight economic progress was offset by the army's expenses. Quite apart from the atrocities committed between 1962 and 1986, which left thousands fatherless, homeless, jobless, dispossessed of their rightful place in society, as well as hundreds of thousands dead, there began a gradual erosion of the way of life that had seemed so hopeful at Independence. Hospitals were looted and hundreds of doctors fled to Kenya and beyond; schools proliferated in areas of political opportunity and some existed only in name, where non-existing teachers drew salaries for doing nothing. Meanwhile real schools had their grants cut and cut - or diverted - and gradually had to ask the parents to produce every single thing the child used in school, from a fork to a light bulb, not to mention his bed and bedding, his desk and chair and all his stationery. Shops almost disappeared, except for expensive boutiques whose owners had acted quickly at the Asian departure and succeeded in making overseas investments to enable them to afford foreign currency. Roadside markets continued much the same, and peasant farmers suffered less than professional people, because they had land and food as before; but all who had to buy food and clothes began to be totally impoverished. The currency was changed three times, and a loaf of bread went from fifty cents to three shillings fifty cents to four hundred shillings. Translated into sterling, it was much the same as costs in UK, but the salary of a teacher was only worth about five loaves a week, with nothing else at all.

This in turn led to people doing more than one job, and when you boarded a taxi you would find it was owned by a pastor or a professor, trying to find the means to keep his children at school. The only way a young man could afford a wedding was to get all his friends to fund-raise for him over several months. As soon as his wedding was over, he would have to do the same for them. It was amazing to see the babies dressed so immaculately, when you realised that they were lucky to have any clothes at all.

Then the educational rat race would begin, and parents would be struggling to send their toddlers to nursery school as the first step on the slippery ladder to university. And all the time the gap between rich and poor grew, for some made the money others lost. Many school children would spend in a week at the tuck shop more than their teachers earned in a month. This led to an exodus of teachers to places with a more friendly economy, where they could at least buy a new shirt and eat properly once a day.

Doctors seemed to be a prime target for political persecution, and hundreds fled for their lives. They served other countries wonderfully. Later, many left highly paid posts overseas and came back to join the poor in Uganda; but in so doing they risked not being able to fund their children's education.

One day in the seventies, a friend of mine who had been a head teacher long before me, said:

"You know, it is becoming quite impossible to run a school under these conditions. I think I shall go home and stay there."

I said: "If you have only just discovered that, you might as well continue." And she did, till she returned from leave one time to find her post filled by a political appointee.

When I began to run the school, I handled about nine hundred thousand shillings annually. When I left eighteen years later it was over a hundred million, and the mind had stopped boggling, because that was only about fifty thousand pounds. Later it was less still. But worse than the cost of things was their absence. The only things that never disappeared from the shops were tea and bananas, while soap, sugar and salt became rarities, leading naturally to black marketing.

When Amin invited Pakistanis to come and fill some of the vacant teaching posts, he had to provide basic food for them, and for two or three years all expatriates could go and purchase generous allowances of sugar, rice, salt, cooking-oil and washing-soap. The allowance was per teacher, so we single people staggered out with kilos of commodities for our friends, and by the time the Pakistanis left, disillusioned, we had found another way of getting these essentials. I was amazed that we were never hijacked carrying it all home, for a needy Ugandan could have made a small fortune reselling it.

Later these basics were sold at parish level, and the teachers we had helped would invariably collect ours for us, hoping maybe to get a little of the supply themselves. I once provided a bag with a small hole in it and a trail of sugar stretched from the headquarters 'shop' to my front door. No Ugandan would have been so casual.

Clothes were prohibitive, but many needs were met by parcels from overseas. Everything, even balaclava helmets, found a welcome home. We used to charge a few shillings to cover transport costs, but we never lost a parcel, despite the value of the contents to people handling them, and never paid any customs either. The real goodies would be put away till Christmas, when each family would receive a bagful of this and that: candles, soap, toys, clothes, knitting wool, vaseline and razor blades, pens and crayons, even exercise books. These were small gifts, but would save hundreds of shillings when the next school term began. A toilet roll or a tube of Colgate was a real luxury.

The most precious commodity of all was water. We had a borehole, pumped by electricity, a good half mile from the school. The pump always failed at a crucial moment, in examination time or when a coup was imminent. Fortunately, the borehole was taken over by decree in Amin's time, though it was miles out of Kampala, so the responsibility for maintenance was not ours. Even so, I fought many a battle to get a repair or a new pump, and we got one literally as an invading army was advancing, though of course the electricity to use it was off by then. So we demanded a tanker, and it came daily, dodging the enemy, till one day the driver produced a demand note for a cool million shillings. I bluffed my way out of that, but could no longer expect the supply from the tanker, and we began the long daily drag up and down the hill to fetch water by hand for over a thousand children, staff families and farm animals. Ugandan children are used to hefting a twenty litre jerrycan on their heads, but it does interrupt studies, as each one would take two or three minutes to fill. I was blessed with two rain tanks and two indoor ones, and seldom ran out, and at such times my popularity rose, especially with the parents of young children. We had to keep one tank for the dining room. The tractor would pull up outside and can after can of water would be poured into drums. Then it would bump its way to the diningroom and men would lift the water up into the tanks there, and come back for more. Any child needing a punishment at such times knew what she would be asked to do!

Living without telephone, regular electricity and water, with basic food supplies by no means certain, and incidents like hijacking of cars and reports of murder all around us, taught us as nothing else could to live a day at a time and to live consciously depending on the protection and provision of God. And sharing what you had, even sharing in sympathy with those who lost what you could not provide for them, broke down many of the barriers there had always been between white and black, old and young, headmistress and staff. It began during the 1979 Liberation War, which for us was a mere month, but a month packed with incident. We had no cash, because the banks closed abruptly as the armies approached Kampala, and we were stuck with several hundred girls even after as many as possible were fetched by parents. We had a drum of petrol, but dared not take a car out of the compound. Our only nurse gave birth to a baby the day the banks closed, and in all five were born on the compound at that time, the last to the qualified midwife who had rescued the others! The local farmers gave us potatoes on credit for the school, but most of the staff had only what the many refugees who filled their houses kindly went out and foraged for. I found a stock of biscuits, matches and such like that we had been persuaded to put aside in an earlier crisis; but as the days went by, I realised that in a week, I would not have a match, a candle or a drop of cooking-oil left, and my water taps would not fill my kettle many more times. The other half of my house contained two families of clergy from Kampala, and they never wavered from the belief that help was on the way. Then one day the influx of refugees stopped, turned round and went home, because they had heard that all empty houses in the city were being looted; and the arrival of the army opened up the roads and the shops and we could use up our supplies again.

It was not only food and water shortages that threw us back on God's mercy. It was lack of communication too. With no telephone, and so many road blocks and threats of hijacking at unofficial ones, we still had to keep in touch with our ministry. But life was as tough for them, so offices tended to close by 3.0 pm. I would save up my problems till I needed to see three or four people, and then set off, to be told on arrival that the first two were in a meeting and wouldn't be out till lunchtime. I would locate the third, but minutes would tick by while he was engaged on the phone. I would go back to the first to find the meeting still on, and in desperation get into the lift to go out. Then the miracle would happen: as the door opened I would find both the men I had come to see getting in, so all I had to do was stay put and follow them to the office, talking as I went. I would then get in without further delay, and see them both. God could always do better than any calculations one tried, and the reasons for seeing the officials were often terribly important, like getting permission to close the school for lack of water, or to take on a teacher for children who had been teaching themselves for a public exam. And it all seemed to be the result of living in trust that each day, somehow, the things that were impossible with man would turn out to be possible with God.

When you are back in England, you wonder if you can really expect God to rescue you in such circumstances, when there is usually some means of transport and communication at hand. But it is still a good way to live, and I got a lift to the airport more than once by simply praying for it. The other side of the story is, of course, that for much of the time you were simply learning patience, when nothing went as planned! When I arrived back at Entebbe once, no-one met me, because no-one could have known I was coming. Uganda Airlines had been for a refit, and we were all kept waiting weeks for a flight. I got on the airport bus, but it was stopped and emptied at every road block, and the twenty mile trip took three hours. But in Kampala, when I was about to begin a long search for someone to take me home with thirty kg of luggage, I walked straight into our bishop, going in that direction and delighted to help. He was going to visit an old lady who had been robbed on our road, and the purple shirt cut out a lot of delay at the road blocks; so the man of God came to the rescue of both of His needy children, without any extra petrol being used.

One is always taught to plan, and from time to time I would forget that it is different in Africa, and look ahead. I would buy in uniform material for a year ahead, only to find the cellar flooded or white ants chewing merrily through the bales; and there was always a risk of theft. Once, I obtained a hundred reams of duplicating paper at a very good price in December when most people were out of funds; but going to the cupboard to get out a ream early the next term, I encountered a sticky mess like sugar, and opening up I found that ants had eaten through the wall, the cupboard and up the middle of ream upon ream. Exam papers had chewed edges for terms and the Sunday school had a pile of scrap to draw on, but the money we had saved was lost. Slowly, we learnt that anything we had should be used. Money, because of inflation, was best turned into something storable and durable and not too easily stolen. Goods were to be distributed. Food was to be eaten, in faith that there would be a new supply before long, for weevils would attack the beans, and rats would get into the storeroom. Books were to be issued. We once had a wonderful supply of books from an overseas government, which some heads decided to sell - maybe to buy food instead. So the inspectors came one day and asked to see our stock. I explained that every single book was in use, and to see them the whole school would have to be called - for no child would risk leaving a textbook in her desk over lunchtime, and it was 1.00 pm when they came. Ruefully, they admitted that books were meant for use and we had certainly made use of them, so they went away to see if they could trap another headmaster. Some of the books, about skiing or metallurgy, were not as useful as others, but we cadged books on home economics from schools that did not teach it, in exchange for those on football or woodwork, and ended up with quite a library on the subject.

Being so short of everything meant that whatever you did acquire would be greeted with delight. We had some American neighbours who used to come to our Sunday services and to coffee afterwards. Hearing us pass round the common bananas with the quip, "Have a biscuit!" they realised that biscuits were just not on the menu, and it was not long before plates of cookies or even a cake would appear for Sunday coffee, for the US workers were not under the same constraints. The delight on everyone's face was reward enough for their kindness. We had some friends who came out every so often to train personnel on behalf of the British Government. They only needed a few clean shirts in their luggage so they would collect up second-hand clothes, toys and packet foods and arrive with a suitcase full when they came to visit; and on return would post piles of letters from the hostesses. The postage in Uganda seemed to be geared to the expatriate business world, not people on allowances, but we seldom had to fork out large sums. Someone would always be a pigeon.

In the end it is all about inter-relatedness and trust, patience and faith. If one can learn that as a way of life, it becomes very exciting, and not in the least frustrating.

In God's economy, there are always enough loaves and fishes.

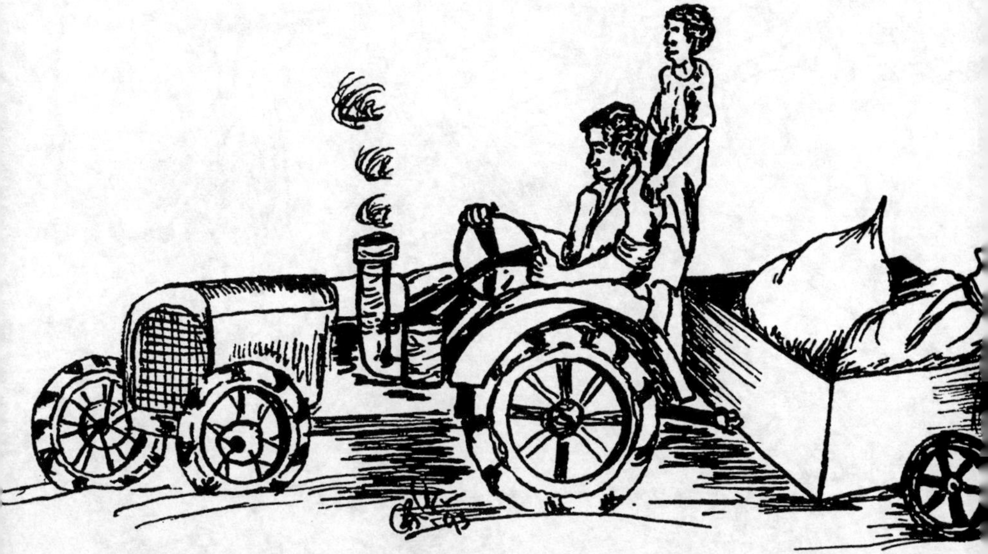

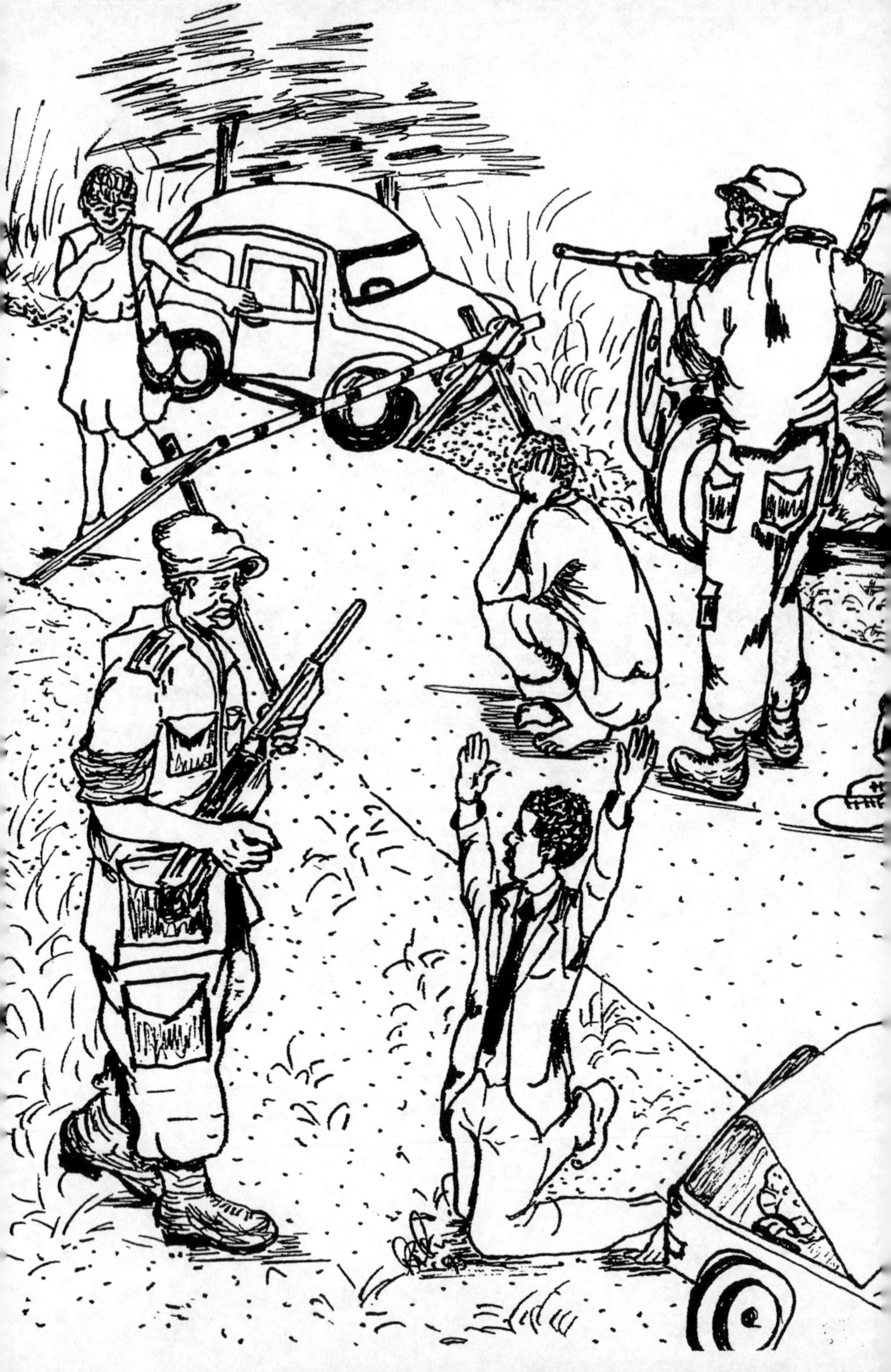

7. IN THE PRESENCE OF MY ENEMIES

Psalm 23 is in constant use in Uganda. It is sung at every wake and funeral, every wedding and at most national services. It is also on every school syllabus at every level, and I used to get my fifteen-year-olds to write their own versions, many of which spoke of God's protection from bullets, from the "Sabasaba" (77) gun of the 1979 war; from dangers on the road and at road blocks; and His provision of every desperate need, from toothpaste, to a new shirt, to a term's fees. Above all was the joy of being free from the fear of death.

Looking back over twenty years of very dangerous living in Uganda, I am amazed at the way in which we were protected. I looked down the barrel of several guns, but on both occasions when I temporarily lost my cars they were taken from me on loan, as a courtesy, and actually returned, battered but repairable. Our school compound, which had no real fence, no locked gates and only a handful of elderly men to guard it at night, was extremely vulnerable. We did have thieves, most likely our employees, and we did have threats, but we lost very little.

Once, during a time of curfew, a young woman teacher was leading evening prayers in a chapel by the light of one candle, when it sounded as if a rain of bullets landed on the roof. We were singing "Trust and obey", and there was just a moment in between a verse and the chorus when it looked as if the girls would all rush out and flee to the dormitories. But the words of the hymn spoke their own message and the singing went on. There was no further noise till the squeals of relief when the service ended. Next day we learnt that the Special Force were chasing a suspect through our compound and fired in the air: a new tin roof echoing the volley explained the terrifying noise. Many people who were not protected as we were, who suffered injury, loss and death of friends and relatives, questioned why we were so blessed. We believe it was partly because we did claim the protection of God and praise him for it, and partly to encourage us to tell others how mighty God's protection can be; this God who in David's picture actually sets up a banqueting table in a place where all our enemies can see us and invites us to sit and eat.

From the mid-sixties to the late eighties, road-blocks were common, set up partly out of fear of subversive activity and partly as a very useful means of supplementing the soldiers' meagre salaries by looting passing vehicles. One of the last such blocks was an apparently official road toll to pay for the splendid new surface gradually taking the place of the ruts and corrugations of the previous ten years. Then one day the government discovered that the toll tickets were being used several times over, that all sorts of unofficial pill-boxes had been put up in residential areas, and that most of the money was going to the pirates. All but the main road tolls disappeared overnight, to our great relief.

The serious road-blocks were quite another thing. Passengers would be herded out of buses, searched, made to open all their bags and often told to lie face down on the ground until it occurred to them to offer a bribe. This could happen many times in one journey. Cars would be stopped and asked for 'coffee', another bribe. Lorries could spend hours at the side of the road waiting to be searched when there was a dearth of cars. Failure to produce a driving licence, a log book, or a poll-tax ticket would lead to a big fine on the spot and possibly detention. Worse still, bandits set up their own road-blocks and took the cars that stopped at gunpoint. Most of the demands would be made in Swahili, which many people didn't understand, though at times it was quite useful to feign incomprehension while you thought out what to say...

I once took my Mini Countryman past a control point:

"Fungua hi!" (Open here)

So I opened the bonnet which he thumped. He was annoyed to behold just an engine.

"Boot where?" I tried to indicate that there was no boot - the back was open to view. Going to the back his eye fell on the jack lever.

"Not allowed!"

But being white I did get away with my jack.

By the time we had learnt the necessary Swahili, they had mastered a few English phrases: "Where from? Where to? Give cigarette! Carr'on." They were as nervous as we were, and the best method was to stop, turn off the ignition, roll down the window and greet first. This seemed to relax them, but some carried out their instructions to the letter. The story goes that one chap made everyone remove their shoes, and when asked why replied, "We told to search every boot."

They had good reason to stop cars, for they often found guns under the seat or in the lining of the doors. At the time when Luwero Triangle was being used as the operations base by Museveni's guerrillas, they kept up communication with the capital very efficiently, however hard Obote's men tried to catch them. A 'business man' would pass the road-block, turn down a side road out of view and change his clothes, so the next check found a farmer. Quite frequently an innocent looking old man's load of charcoal would be searched, and found to be too heavy and to contain guns.

Road-blocks on the way from the airport were among the strictest. Having just been through customs, you would be stopped, and greedy eyes would peruse the new clothes brought in from London or New York. Some nervous new arrivals would part with a few treasures; we used to say ours were already promised, and make a big point of being teachers and not tourists. At the Kampala end of the road they could be very brusque, and once a dark-haired friend of mine could not find her licence when challenged to produce it. As the demand grew more menacing I remembered that the photo on mine was taken twenty years ago so I produced it and we were immediately told "Carr'on." Some way further on we drew up by the roadside for a good laugh, but it had not seemed amusing at the time.

When my Ugandan driver was in the car on his own he did not have such an easy time. Twice he returned hours later than expected having been arrested for parking in the wrong place, when all he had done was to slow down to avoid an obstruction in the road. He was taken to court and relieved of one thousand shillings. Once he went to collect day-old chicks from the airport and unfortunately chose a Coup Day to do so. He got the chicks all right and was then hijacked by soldiers for about fifteen miles. At the next road-block some others forced him to drive all the way back to the airport, and he then found himself in a checking queue, which made him fear for the car, let alone the chicks. So he calmly drove to the front of the queue, looked as determined as possible and was waved on: someone assumed he had been passed. He found a place to spend the night off the road, watered the chicks and eventually turned up at school twenty-seven hours after setting out on a three hour ploy. Incredibly, not a single chick died.

Arrests did not always take place at road-blocks. Two young

English staff were foolhardy enough to visit a local bar with their African girl-friends and were arrested as 'guerrillas'. I had to search for their passports and go and bail them out from the Central Police Station. They learnt to be more circumspect after that. Our farm manager was attacked and killed in what seemed to be a marital squabble, and a young teacher was accused of murdering him. He was in great danger of disappearing for good inside a police station, as I could tell from the extreme annoyance shown when I insisted on escorting him there and waiting throughout the interrogation. In the end he had to leave the country: it became too hot to stay.

One morning I was informed that three of our nightwatchmen had been arrested at the gate as they went off duty at 6.00 am. They had been relieved of their wellingtons, their torches and their ID cards and put in a police cell. When I went to the police station to request their release, I was told they had been taken by the army, and I could go to Kitii and see the officer there if I dared. At that moment he arrived at the police post, so I went with him. We drove along a rutted, weedy murram road, with elephant grass several feet high on either side, showing that cultivation had been abandoned. The officer tried to convince me that the ten thousand shillings ransom being demanded was just a test of their genuineness. If they came back with it they were not guerrillas. Looking out of the window at the deserted fields and disused road, I thought that if I were a Ugandan nothing would persuade me to go on foot alone along such a road. In any case ten thousand shillings was three months' salary.

Kitii used to be a small trading centre halfway between two main roads. As we drew up outside what had been a small shop, I realised the place was now a barracks, and apart from the soldiers noisily playing cards, there was not a soul in sight. I began to feel a little nervous, but in five minutes or so the officer returned and held out the three ID cards.

"Look," he said, "they haven't even taken the five shilling note out of this one."

No mention was made of about six thousand shillings worth of boots and torches, but it was the men I was rescuing, not the boots.

The journey back to the police station was somehow lighter and shorter than the foray into the bush, and the OC Police was clearly relieved that we were back and that he could now release the men. I asked him why he had not checked with the school whether the men were likely to be suspect, since we could easily have vouched for them. He gave me a look which said I must have come from another world. The police did not argue with the army, no matter what they did.

There is no doubt that only a white face could have got to Kitii and back that day, and white faces were needed all too often in those days to ensure school supplies and safe passage for our lorry and even our girls; and white faces were known not to offer bribes, so we could save money too. At one end of term, when the road-blocks were very severe, I went on the lorry with the girls who were not fetched and leant out of the window at every stop; it worked wonders. Long after the military checks were removed, there was still a curfew on lorries, which were not supposed to move after dusk. We were bringing home a party of sixth formers from about seventy miles away and drew up at 6.55 pm to be told we would have to stay there overnight. We were in the centre of Kampala, and it took even the white face some time to convince the police that it was not a suitable venue for fifty teenage girls. He let us go and then we realised that two more check-points had to be passed.

"We shall have to pray," said the geography teacher in charge of the outing. We drew up at 7.10 at a row of spikes, and I leant out ready to plead with the policeman on duty. He was so startled at seeing an elderly white woman in a lorry at all that without a word he waved us on.

After the episode of the murdered farm manager, our watchmen were severely beaten up under interrogation and some were too sick to work, while others left our employment. Who can blame them? One night the headman came to tell me that he was alone on duty and he wasn't well, so we divided the night between us. I couldn't help smiling to think of all the potential thieves who didn't know that one middle-aged European woman was their only threat.

One night when there were hostile forces around, a landrover full of soldiers roared up to the gate. The gateman, terrified, took refuge in the carpenter's store just behind his post and waited for the shouts and shots he expected.

Nothing happened. Dead silence. So he crept out and saw the vehicle through what looked like a wall of fire. The silence remained for about a minute and then the landrover reversed some distance down the road, turned and roared off.

Awe-struck, the man reported, "It was an angel, I tell you. I cannot explain otherwise how that car went away just like that."

One night I had to take a dying man to hospital. The roadblocks were at their rudest, roughest and greediest, but we had to go. On the way in, it was easy to put on the light and reveal the patient lying along the back of the car, but having left him at the hospital, there would be no such proof of our mission on the way home.

As we drove out of the hospital, a landrover I hadn't seen

before followed us, and it drove with headlights full on us for several miles till we both stopped at the road block. The soldiers approached the landrover, not our car, then waved us both on with no questioning, and the bright light went out as the following car turned off to the right. Next day I looked for the turning. There was no turning off on that stretch of the road. Angels again? I believe so, and I believed it all the more when my neighbour described the abusive treatment she had had at that very road block.

Whenever I drove or escorted the dead or dying in those days I used to sing silently or aloud, depending on the company: "The Lord's my shepherd... Yea though I walk through death's dark vale, yet will I fear none ill." Never was I more conscious of the presence of the shepherd than that dark night. A few nights later, I dreamt that I was escorting a coffin on a plane and it was in the middle of the aisle, so you could not avoid seeing it. I looked in to see whose body it was - that very man - and at the foot of the coffin stood the devil himself, leering at me. I woke up trembling, and glad to find it was a dream, but it was one of several experiences that taught me that God is there in the fear - He does not remove or prevent fearful happenings.

It was March 1979, and the Liberation Army, which had advanced on foot to deliver Uganda from Idi Amin's Regime, was already near Kampala. Many of our schoolgirls had been fetched home by car, borrowed ambulance, hired lorry or even wheelbarrow, their parents preferring to have the family all together since their immediate future was uncertain. Some of the forty-strong classes were down to fifteen or twenty, but lessons continued, with helicopters passing the windows of the upstairs classrooms uncomfortably close. They were actually full of wounded Libyan mercenaries, but they looked threatening. Many of the children's homes were on the far side of the fighting line, and the teachers said they would rather work than sit and imagine what might be happening to their homes. We were cut off from the bank and already buying food from local farms on credit:

"You may pay afterwards," said the farmers. "The army will just help themselves."

I carried around all day a clipboard with the six hundred students' names, and marked off those who were fetched; but I was in the office when a tired old man on a bicycle rode up, propped his machine against the wall, and proffered a small damp note on which was scribbled in pencil in the local language:

"If my daughter is safe with you, keep her. If not, send her home with this man."

"Home" meant forty miles on the back of the bicycle, and it was raining. I called the girl, made sure she knew the man, and asked her if she was willing to go with him. She looked very doubtful, and without stopping to consider the implications, I found myself writing:

"She's quite safe with us, so we are keeping her here." As the old man rode off, I realised that I had committed myself to protecting this fourteen-year-old girl in a situation which was totally unpredictable. Somehow the act of writing that note convinced me that I should be able to keep my promise to the mother.

A few days later, we were rehearsing a play for Good Friday in the chapel when a startled looking schoolgirl appeared in the doorway and mouthed:

"Your visitors are outside," and disappeared up the drive.

I went out to find two young soldiers fingering their guns

rather awkwardly. Their story was that Amin had given them permission to take their families to safety before the final battle and they needed transport. They asked to 'borrow' my car. Realising that they would take someone's vehicle anyway, I went to fetch my twenty year-old Mini, stopping on the way to phone the police to ask them to intercept it. The soldiers expressed gratitude and promised to return the car "Very soon, Madam." They even offered to sign for it.

Next day half the village came to commiserate with me on the loss of my car, using the same language as is used when they come to console the bereaved:

"Nga kitalo!" (What a shame) "Ng'olabye!" (You have seen sorrow). Once again from inner conviction I assured them that my car would come back.

For a week it was seen being used as a taxi on the local roads and the police were too scared to confiscate it; but the next Saturday it came back - with a puncture, no petrol in the tank and the exhaust pipe broken off, but still my car.

"You see we have returned it, Madam, just as we promised!"

This time the "Nga kitalo!" meant, "What a wonder."

I heard of hundreds of vehicles taken at gunpoint, often with bloodshed, and never seen again - but mine came back.

Four days after that I was teaching the sixth form Shakespeare when the office manager came for me:

"There are fifteen armed men at the office demanding the bus." By this time we had learnt that the Liberators had a device which could detect the presence of even four armed men, and strike, and here were four times that number. They must be got rid of fast! So I rapidly escorted them to the bus shelter and handed them the keys. The bus was fairly new and our pride and joy, but I couldn't see it go fast enough with two hundred girls in the place.

Two of them climbed in and tried the engine. Nothing happened.

"Where is the driver?"

"About four miles away. He doesn't work afternoons at present."

"Oh, well how far is it to Bombo?" (The nearest barracks).

"Only seven miles across country. Let me show you the short cut."

So it was that the bizarre procession of weary soldiers, in a motley collection of army, police and schoolboy caps, carrying guns, grenades and stolen radios and escorted by a few brave members of staff who decided to die with me, crossed the games field to the gate of the next-door farm, where they walked off, the bus apparently forgotten.

As we walked back, unable to believe our deliverance from what could have been an ugly encounter, we saw someone waving and shouting at us, "The war is over! Kampala has fallen! Call them back!"

But they had done us no harm. Three times over in a few days we had seen God in control of his children. We let them go. In the days that followed I learnt that among the faces that filled the dormitory windows near the bus shelter were many praying for our safety. I also discovered that the driver had removed the rotor arm from the bus; and people said the young soldiers had only half a gun each when they came for the car.

At the time I knew none of these things. I only knew God's peace - a sense of being held in the hollow of his hand.

It was February 1988 and Princess Anne was coming to visit the school. After much excitement and many hours of preparation, someone came to inspect where she would actually sit in my 1908 mud-brick sitting room. The corner they preferred was beneath an ominous crack in the ceiling, which our welcoming drums might well loosen, so I insisted that she sit with her back to the window in order to be able to see the people being presented to her.

Then I realised that that position looked straight along to the bullet hole in the ceiling! In the event, she didn't appear to notice.

The bullet hole got there one Sunday morning in 1985. We had just held a lovely service at the back of the chapel, two days after the latest Liberation when the forces of Yoweri Museveni reached Kampala. The girls had got home in the nick of time, for lorries full of soldiers arrived only minutes after the last buses and taxis reached the city. As the service ended we heard a lot of vehicle noise. Then we saw the Sunday School children who had been playing outside the chapel scatter in alarm. A few minutes later I was beckoned out: "Soldiers in your house, carrying out saucepans and things! Come quick!"

I went up with a colleague and found just that. In typical school-teacher fashion I asked:

"What do you think you are doing?"

Very, very drunk voices replied:

"We're the Ll-liberatorssh! Come to-uk-liiiberate you all!"

"Shoot them..No, tie them up while we search! ...Better not shoot. They're white teachers. Our children need them. If we kill them, where will we get more?

"Desperately, I remember saying over and over the theme of our service: The Lord Reigns, and then asking them:

"Who are you liberating and from what?"

"Liiiberators, thatsh what we are, Liilliberators." Conversation and repartee were proving difficult, when suddenly an officer appeared in the doorway, rather less drunk.

"Put that gun down or I'll shoot you!"

Then it happened. Frustrated beyond control, the soldier who stood just between us, less than two feet away, suddenly fired his rifle into the ceiling above our heads. My first thought was, "The ceiling will now fall and how shall I get it repaired?" But all I said was, "What was that for?"

It released the tension inside the house, but alarmed the congregation in church and those still in the chapel. "Someone's dead in the HM's House. Perhaps she's the one," was the common thought.

"No.. There are two pairs of white legs still standing up," was the news relayed from someone hiding behind a tree.

It was several days before visits from these soldiers stopped, and in due course they looted cars and beat up the gatekeeper for delaying their arrival or departure. But that day they drove off, leaving behind all the loot except two loaves of bread and an alarm clock, which were after all replaceable... and the bread would soak up some of the excess beer they had consumed.

By March 1986 such confrontations were much more uncommon and in the years that followed the only hostile visitors I had to deal with were disappointed parents or government officials who couldn't get places in school for the asking. In some ways they were harder to deal with.

The hole in the ceiling is still there, a timely reminder that we had a close brush with death, but also that once again, when we were helpless God held back our foes.

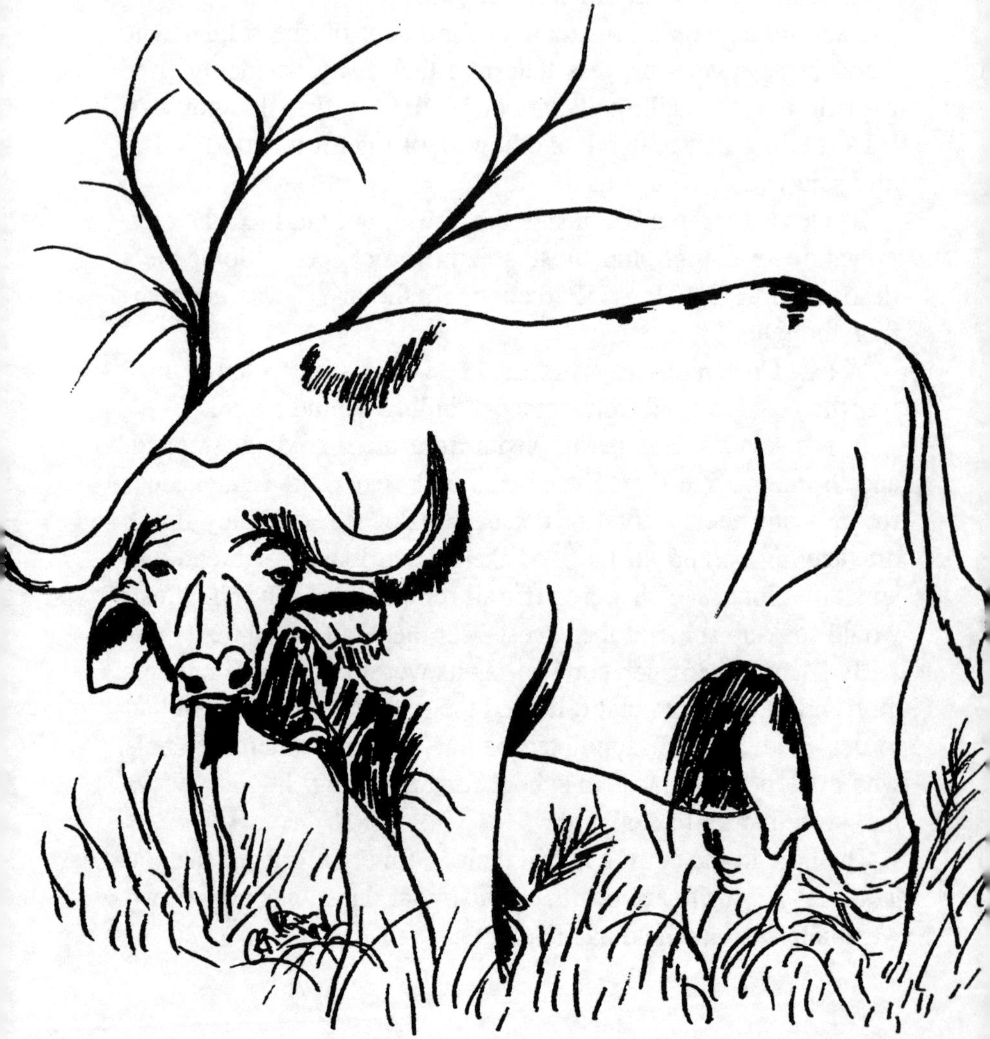

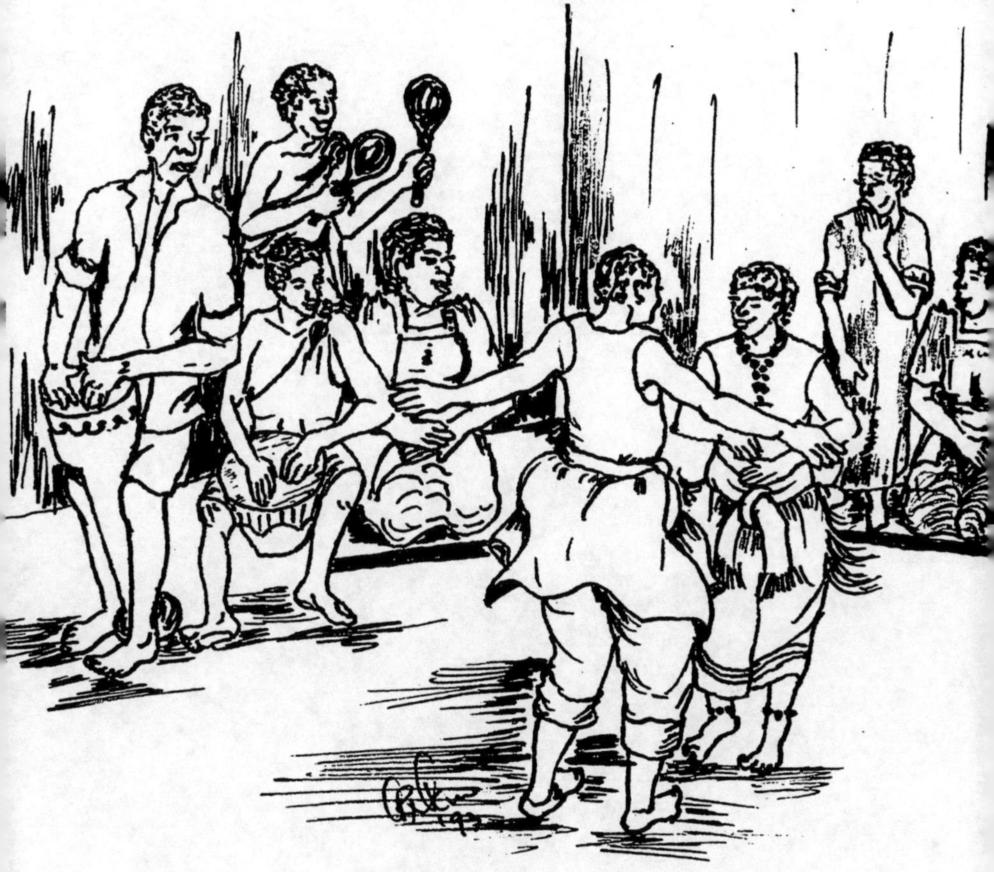

8. SING A NEW SONG

It is early October. A group of girls, dressed in uniforms with coloured cloths draped over their shoulders, are waiting excitedly in a teacher's garden. On the lawn round the corner stand four drums of different shapes and sizes and a large African xylophone, some shakers and small gourds and a cow horn. The day has come for the O level practical music examination for thirty of the country's total of about eighty candidates.

Before these instruments come into play, each of the girls will go in and perform her Western pieces, singing or playing either the recorder or the piano. A few schools may have other instruments, like trumpets or horns, but few can afford them or find a teacher. These will be of grade four or above, and many will only have learnt the piano since they joined secondary school. Singing, for most of them, comes naturally, but not necessarily Western style.

Later in the day, each will sing songs from several different parts of Uganda and explain them. The rest of the group will form the chorus and provide the accompaniment on the drums. Those who choose drumming will have to play all four drums efficiently, and explain how they are made and used. So will the performers on the xylophone, which is made of soft wooden bricks of varying sizes and beaten with sticks. One player makes the melody and the other, who counts as accompanist, beats a steady rhythm on the other side. They usually sit on the ground on either side of it.

The exam will take all day, and by the end every technique of touch, tone, drama and interpretation will have been demonstrated. What is more, another milestone will have been passed in the attempt to maintain the best of Uganda's culture among those who will go furthest in the education system. A few will take music at A level also, but so far that is entirely Western in content, as no one has found a way to make the testing of African music at that level hard enough. Those who go on to study music at the university complain that they are back in the middle school!

A few months earlier, many schools will have taken part in the National Music Festival where all kinds of pieces are judged including original compositions using the whole range of African instruments, and dances from different regions, in full costume. Problems of transport and timing across other activities, and the fact that some schools with music seriously on their curriculum have a distinct advantage, discourage some from attending; but when all is well organised it is a very exciting occasion, and a great encouragement to national prestige. For there is no denying the rich variety and power of the musical traditions of Uganda.

In 1964, a troupe called "Heartbeat of Africa" was formed, with the idea of taking Ugandan culture abroad, and including in the repertoire music from every tribe. At the same time our school was preparing an entertainment for the opening of a new building, and had the same idea. Instead of a group from Buganda doing their dance, followed by a song from Acholi and then a dance from Rwanda, the same group would learn all the songs and dances and perform each other's. Roars of laughter greeted the first attempts of the southerners trying to waggle their necks as only the Acholi can, and when the mixed group tried to emulate the gracefulness of the Banyarwanda they looked more like elephants. But it was a step towards respect for one another's culture and enormously enriching and great fun. "Nakalema and the Crane'', as the opera was called, was shown only to that audience, but it started a tradition of mixing tribal songs and dances that was good in every way. We smiled when we realised that we were doing the same thing as "Heartbeat".

For the different regions of Uganda have very distinct musical traditions: there is really no such thing as Ugandan culture. What the regions have in common is that music is an integral part of life and is used on many different occasions. Any area that ever had a king will have court music; every region has dances for weddings and feasts and festivals; every region has its own costumes and traditions about who plays which instruments. But the details will vary. Drums, hollowed out from trees, will be made of the trees which grow around and be covered with the hides of local cattle, and so on. And yet there is a curious similarity even between East and West Africa in some instruments. One thing you may be sure of is that they will be locally handmade, not mass-produced. If you want a new drum, you must ask for it months in advance to allow for all the processes involved in the making: finding the tree, cutting it down, drying it out, carving the shape, and preparing the hide before it is attached to form the beating surface.

Some practical reasons arose when dances from the remote rural areas first came to the stage of the National Theatre. Girls did not wear bras at home. Would an international audience be shocked, or worse, despise them if they appeared with naked tops? For fear of the latter reaction, the girls were clad accordingly, but part of their "culture" was lost in the process. When Acholi dancers blow horns or bang gourds, the noise travels for miles in the open air: inside a theatre it was deafening and troubled an audience not yet attuned to the decibels of modern music. Some dances, when brought indoors and away from their natural context, can appear offensively explicit; so there is some watering down when upcountry comes to town. But a start has been made, and any fear of the culture being swallowed up or obliterated by Western culture has gone.

Music comes instinctively to Ugandans. Sing them a new tune, and by the third rendering it is complete with parts, and by the fourth accompanied with drums and shakers, and imbued with a rhythm its composer never thought of. Teaching a high standard of Western music in that environment therefore has its problems, but there is no difficulty with speed of learning. When our choir came to Britain in 1963 they were able to sing a Cathedral Evensong despite never having sung pointed psalms before, and when they found a new hymn on one church board and asked for a chance to learn it they amazed the organist by picking it up after one play through. Music is at the heart of life in Uganda, so for every occasion it provides a means of expression, whether of grief or exuberant joy. When anyone performs, there is immediate response and identification and applause at the end. Because so much music had pagan origins and significance, the churches began by condemning it; but it has gradually been 'baptised', as it were. In many churches drums and shakers are now acceptable in a service, not just as a means of calling people to church or keeping the beat steady when there is no organ or piano.

Soon after the final Liberation of Kampala in 1986, when many children were left parentless, one orphanage decided that the children themselves should earn their school fees and their keep by touring abroad as a choir. This they did. Some of the money they raised was no doubt given out of sympathy for their plight, but they put on a superb show. We, too, took our Christian Club choir, not to raise money but to share the Good News, on a three week tour of England and Ireland. What was significant musically about that was that all the songs in English had been composed by members of the choir. Two events encouraged the beginning of these compositions. One was the competition organised by the Good News Bible promoters, "Sing Good News". We heard about it just as we were emerging from the '79 war, but we encouraged girls to try, and sent off our tape with little hope that it would arrive or that its quality would be good enough for anyone to listen to it. To our amazement all the songs we sent were included, so composing went on. Another incentive was that we had sung a certain musical all round Kampala, and everyone had heard us and they were clamouring for more. We could not find another suitable one so our musical director challenged us to write our own. We composed not one but three in the end; and so began a ministry that reached its climax when we were invited to come and sing in Britain in 1983. Since British people wanted some Ugandan music, we prepared a number of traditional songs too; but the songs in English were composed by quite young girls as well as more experienced music scholars.

Music really is the lifeblood of many Ugandans. There is no occasion involving celebrities which is complete without a troupe of singers and dancers. Once they get going there is no stopping them. Everyone gets lost in the movement and noise, joining in the clapping, if not the dancing. Members of Parliament would be considered very stand-offish if they did not join in at least one of the dances performed in their honour; and some of the audience will come forward in the middle of a dance and stuff money down the costume of a dancer, capering round them to get the chance. To keep it up for the length of time the professionals do needs great stamina, but no-one minds if you fall over in the attempt. At a gathering with many tribes it will be a matter of honour for the audience to participate when their own tribal dance comes on; but nowadays they will try the others as well. The dances may look easy and effortless, but they are intricate and exhausting. The songs are usually performed in a semi-circle. The soloist walks or dances or runs from left to right, telling the story of the hunt or the famine or the courtship he has been engaged in, miming dramatic illustrations. Sometimes he is joined by another soloist. The people in the semi-circle clap and drum at his command, and repeat a chorus line, following the mood of the narrative. Towards the end you feel the climax coming, when everyone will stop dead on the same beat. Quite often the soloist plants his foot on the biggest drum as his final note. Many performers seem to have difficulty in stopping, and the song goes on and on as if the climax had got lost. When the Baganda do their courtly dance, they perform consciously to the chief guest, falling flat on their faces before him at the start; and as the dance proceeds, members of the chorus seize horns or come and prance round the younger dancers, encouraging them to get more and more energetic and excited, so that by the end the whole village seems to be involved.

There are, of course, professional music groups, such as the Nyonza and Kampala Singers, who achieve international reputations, and almost every educated Ugandan can join in the Hallelujah Chorus. Those who study abroad usually amaze their fellow students by the ease with which they pick up a Latin motet or an Italian aria. They sing by ear and impress foreign musicians by their accuracy and talent. But it still remains true that spontaneous singing whenever the occasion demands or allows is the greatest gift of Ugandans. They don't need a piano or an organ or even a guitar, though they welcome many indigenous instruments for the purpose. It is exciting to watch the variety of harps and fiddles that adorn many a home actually being played in concert as seriously as drums are. Every year the possibilities increase and the range of instruments widens.

Drama comes equally naturally to Ugandans, though on the whole they prefer to make it up as they go along, and learning words, quick though they are, is a tough discipline. In boarding schools on a Saturday afternoon you will often watch groups of students entertaining their friends with more or less impromptu drama. However much time has been spent rehearsing, the words will be different at the performance, and so, quite often, will the costumes. I remember the agony suffered by a very meticulous wardrobe mistress when the crown or the topee belonging to a second play came on in the village scene in the first, usually on the head of the chief clown. Learning words of a Shakespeare play proved difficult, not because the memories were at fault, but because impromptu drama is the tradition, and it feels unnatural to make prepared speeches. The same problem, incidentally, affects sermons and political speeches, because the ad-libbing will almost always be longer than the text.

Between them, the schools must have acted all the well-known Shakespeare plays for one another, and the language presented no more difficulty than that of any other English dramatist. The National Theatre, forty years old now, has put on remarkable performances from all over the world, but I suspect that where drama has done the most for the people is in the makeshift local theatres, where plays are staged in barns and warehouses, in vernacular languages and on topical themes. Politics was a dangerous game for many decades, but the theatres seemed to be places where corruption could be exposed and grievances aired even in the most unhealthy periods. I once took a class to see a

West African play whose theme was precisely topical and very near the bone; but it did not seem to occur to the Powers that Be that it had any relevance to them. A student whispered to me, "Is this play saying what I think it is?" I had to beg her to keep her thoughts to herself till we got safely away from the theatre. You might even find the A level exam paper requiring students to apply the message of a play to the present situation; but the students would avoid the question, not knowing who would mark the papers.

Each Christmas our first-year students, aged thirteen or so, would produce their own Nativity play, often writing songs to include; and the chapel choir would act as a supplement only, for the whole class had to take part - one hundred and thirty in all. The simplicity of it spoke to all, and we usually had the most recently arrived baby for Jesus. One year when we had a little brother up there, Joseph was asked the child's name, and pronounced very clearly:

"His name is Jesus."

A loud protest was heard at the back of the chapel:

"That's not Jesus, that's my bruvver Paul!"

Another year the table in the chancel became the carpenter's bench, and Joseph was ragged very crudely about marrying a girl who was obviously pregnant; and later in the play the young shepherds came carrying a packet of biscuits and singing, "Happy birthday to you". The kings would be dressed differently each year, in garments created from our cast off long dresses or the contents of aid parcels. Most of our acting cupboard dated back to the 1950's, but some got eaten by cockroaches or were lent and never returned.

In some years Easter was early enough to fall in term time, and then it was the turn of the senior classes to put on a passion play. This they did with amazing sensitivity and realism. We normally used a text this time, as some improvised language can be unintentionally funny. There was no shyness or inhibition about acting the part of Jesus or Judas. There used to be some objections about staying at school for Easter, but afterwards all agreed that it had been a wonderful experience, and for many it was the play that spoke to their hearts, rather than the service.

At 4.00 am on Easter morning the teachers would be woken to the strains of "Up from the grave he arose", sung outside the window by the chapel choir, dressed in white sheets and carrying candles. After an hour or so, half the school would have joined in the procession, but the first sudden burst of song was magical. In the evening, we sometimes produced an Easter play, shorter but exciting. One year, when the girls kept being fetched home just as they had learnt their parts - for it was when Amin's downfall was imminent - the staff took the parts. That has never been forgotten, and we enjoyed it as much as the incredulous audience.

Ugandans can listen for hours to political speeches and sermons: a meeting is not considered very serious if it does not go on long enough for the last late comer to arrive and still hear most of it. But even so, the message seems to be much more indelible if it is acted, sung or danced.

Most of life was dramatised, not always seriously, and one came to enjoy the procedure as much as Ugandans did. I remember being congratulated by an old girl who remembered my first halting attempts to speak Luganda, when she overheard me on the office doorstep berating a chap who was trying to cheat the school. I was so engrossed in the argument that the language came instinctively. One would go to a funeral and watch people put on a convincingly mourning expression while they exchanged the conventional phrase of sympathy, "Nga kitalo!", only to see them a moment later doubled up with laughter as they shared a joke. It was not insincerity, but the conventional part was superbly acted. For many, loud wailing and a good deal of histrionics were expected when bad news was received, and no doubt it released pent up feelings; but only people with an instinct for drama could switch immediately to another mood and mode of expression so naturally. It probably explains why they could act the Passion so movingly. Most were totally unselfconscious, and producing a play in Uganda was one of the most enjoyable experiences I remember, not least because so much of what we rehearsed had been felt on their pulses.

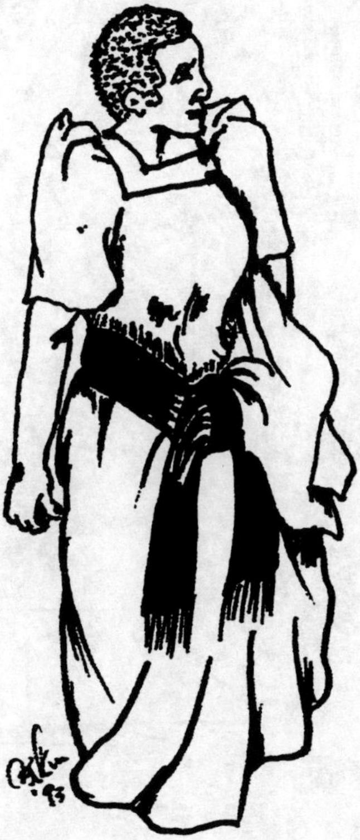

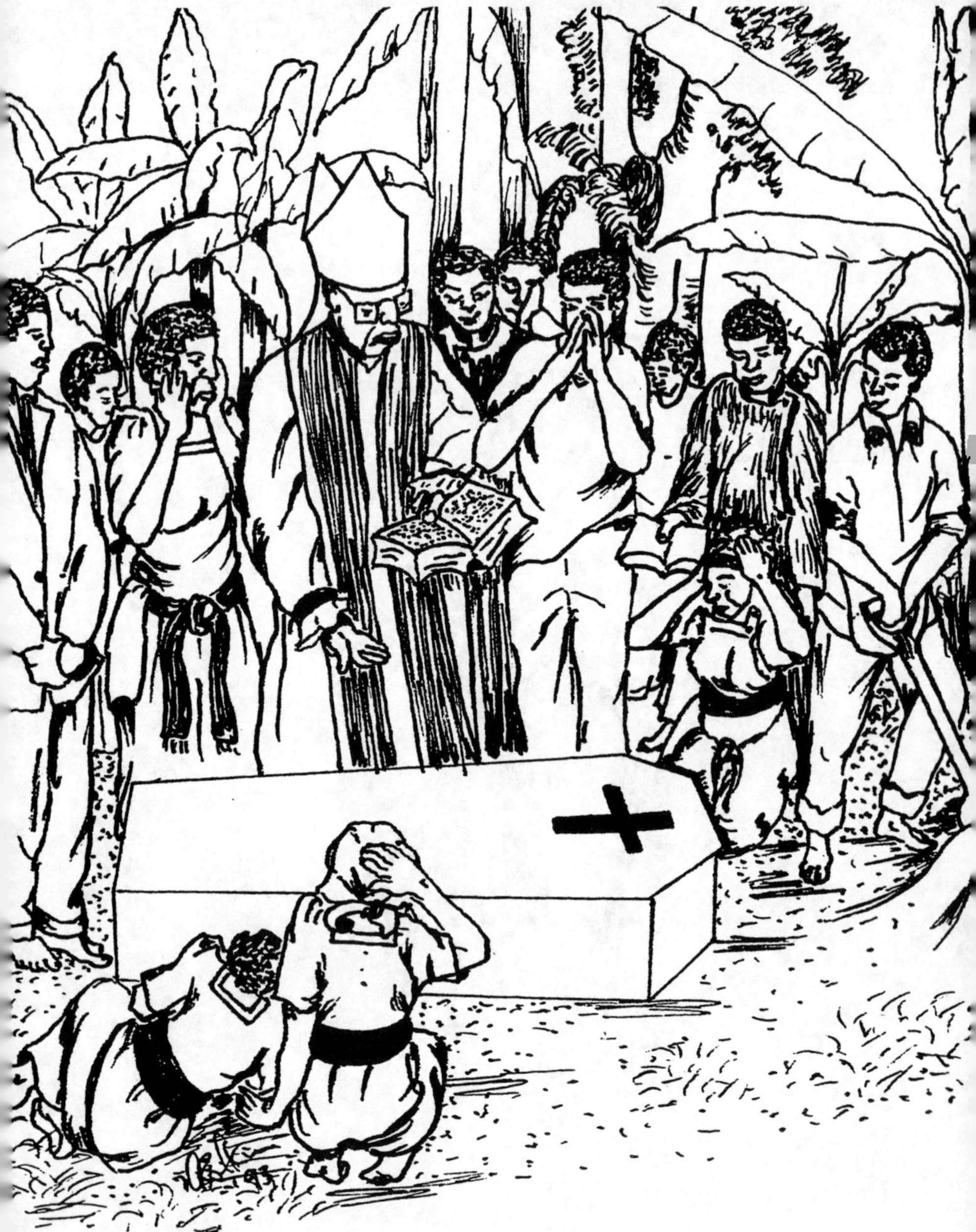

9. BE FAITHFUL UNTO DEATH

"Be faithful unto death and I will give you the crown of life."

The story of the church in Uganda begins with martyrdom and has tended to continue that way, especially in the years since Independence.

When Bishop Hannington was on his way to Buganda, just eight years after the first missionaries were welcomed by the King Mutesa I, he did not know, and neither did the other white men, that there was a saying that whoever came to Buganda by way of Busoga - that is by land from the East - was coming to "eat" Buganda. When his arrival at that point, actually the source of the Nile, was reported to Mutesa's successor, King Muwanga, he immediately ordered his murder, and although many tried to persuade him that the man was no threat to him, and though they delayed the execution as long as they dared in the hopes that he would change his mind, Hannington and most of his company were speared to death on October 29 1885, and during the following year many more martyrs to the Christian faith were speared, beheaded or slowly burnt to death around Kampala at this king's command. Their deaths were not only glorious for their courageous witness at the time; they were very effective in bringing more converts, and within a few years the churches, both Roman Catholic and Protestant, had peace, and education and medical services were soon established.

But death and funerals are a prominent part of life in Uganda, especially now when at least six people in one rural archdeaconry are buried every day after dying of AIDS, which is proving a deadly scourge of the younger generation. In the seventies and early eighties people used to rejoice when their folk died "in the old way" of sickness rather than at the hands of the government thugs; now they rejoice when they die of any other cause than AIDS. Whatever the cause of death, it is important for everyone possible to be at the funeral, and especially the burial. The funeral follows hard upon the death, so most days there is a long list on the radio of those who have "passed away", and the ceremony will be on the following day, probably miles away near the family home. The wealthy may be able to arrange a service in the town and then take the body home for burial, but most people have to hire what vehicle they can, find the money somehow, and go straight along the main road home. The burial will be in the family banana or coffee garden, and all the neighbours will be sure to help dig the grave, for fear no-one will dig theirs if they don't. Burials are usually at 2.0 pm, when it is either pouring with rain or very hot indeed, and despite the sadness of the occasion, one cannot but notice the peace and beauty of the final resting place.

As you arrive, there will be a table set up and some people collecting contributions towards the funeral expenses, which are substantial when you consider the cost of the transport, often hired, and the many expecting to be fed for several days; for as soon as the news of the death is announced, by radio or drums, people gather to sit, and will stay all night and on till the time of the funeral if they can. If the friends are Christians they will sing hymns; if not, there may be a lot of wailing, which may not be altogether sincere, since it is a custom, not an expression of personal grief. At the graveside, the donors will all be thanked; every detail of the sickness or other cause of death will be given in a blow by blow account, and so will the life history of "The Late", whether he was a rascal or a government minister or a bishop. Then the clergy will preach and take their time over it, although everyone is standing. If the congregation is made up of believers, the sermon may be reassuring; if not, it will be a serious call to repent and beware of meeting death unprepared. There is none of the pious wishful-thinking that the departed has "gone to heaven" if it was clear from his lifestyle that he probably hasn't. Ugandan clergy don't usually mince their words.

When the last spadeful is on, the company disperse, apart from the family and the cadgers who hope for yet another free meal. In local custom the family gather some time later for the last funeral rites, but the Christian church regards them as pagan and tries to turn the naming of the heir into something that can be included in the funeral itself. People put on their oldest clothes to attend funerals, and it is hard to tell a minister from a peasant; the ladies wear old busuutis and always a long cloth round their hips; but every passer-by will stop and watch, so there may be schoolchildren in uniforms as well. The poor are buried rolled up in barkcloth; the better off will have coffins and the gravesides will be cemented as well the top.

The desire and necessity for everyone to attend a funeral does produce problems when you are running a boarding school, and I was often considered unfeeling when I discouraged more than half the staff from going to one nearby. We often said among ourselves that the Baganda seemed to have more concern for the dead than the living.

Yet, despite the hasty preparations and all the abuses that funerals in Uganda were open to, they were strangely reassuring occasions. The crowds of supporters, the selfless way in which neighbours would spend days of their time and dig deep into their resources, spoke of a kind of sense of community that you would not see outside Africa; and the Christian answer to death could be made very clear. Somehow the amount of time and effort expended helped the mourners to feel very much upheld and comforted.

But the funerals we experienced were not always mere courtesies. When I had been in Uganda a few months only, the mother of one of the girls in my class died in hospital, and there was no way her body could be taken home to Gulu, so the local clergy buried her on a small plot of land just outside the school gates. The girl was all alone, with very few tribesmates to share her grief, and no-one familiar with the local customs that should have been observed. Later the two tribes involved were to become bitter enemies, but there the grave remains, alongside those of the church dignitaries for whom the land is designated.

In the same plot, equally unofficially, lies the body of our beloved cook, Peter. Peter's wife had typhoid, so he was told to stay away from the kitchen to avoid bringing infection. One evening he went out to his vegetable plot and saw a Special Force soldier snooping about; the next moment he was shot. A neighbour sneaked on to a bicycle and rushed to tell us. We took the lorry and drove fairly nervously, hooting as we went to show that we were not trying to hide. He was hoisted aboard and we drove back to the school clinic. But he had lost too much blood and died a few minutes later. We dared not make the journey again to his rather isolated farm, so he too was buried just outside the gates, this time by the bishop himself.

One year when road-blocks were very tight we had the prettiest little twelve-year-old in the school, probably our youngest. About three weeks into term, she walked into the school dispensary and fell into the nurse's arms. They didn't tell me they feared she was dead, so we tore to the hospital, but too late. It was extremely difficult to get a post-mortem because all the medical students were doing their finals; it was also very dangerous to travel the two hundred miles to her home, but somehow all was arranged and I had to go along and escort her body back to the parents, full of misgivings because her death was a mystery and death in Uganda is always someone's fault. It was May, the rainy season, and the roadsides were fresh and lovely, and we had an army escort (somehow a relative had been found who was a captain and had considerable authority). So every time we approached a road-block everyone stood aside and waved us on. It was like taking royalty home rather than a dead child. When we explained to the parents all we knew, they accepted it without any question, and thanked us for coming and treated us with gentle courtesy. Later we learnt that she had been in a car accident and had probably had some internal injury that was not realised, but the whole experience was less one of grief than of wonder. So many people put themselves to so much trouble to provide a royal homecoming for the child that you could not but think that she was also welcomed like that into heaven.

State funerals took place in Namirembe Cathedral, and when Amin murdered Archbishop Janani Luwum on 16 February 1977, just as the Church of Uganda was celebrating its Centenary, everyone assumed that he would be buried in the cathedral grounds like his predecessors. The grave was dug, but the authorities refused to release his body. This was mainly because he had died of bullet wounds fired by Amin himself and not - as the radio wanted us to believe - in a car accident when he was trying to escape from his guards. So there could be no funeral, but come Sunday there was a service anyway so we took two or three car loads of staff and attended the service. At first we had to stand outside but later someone found us places. The Holy Communion service proceeded as usual, but the hymns were all about martyrs. Slowly the congregation realised that we were in fact holding Janani's Memorial but in such a way that no one could take exception to it. As the service ended, everyone went out singing the hymn known as the martyrs' hymn because it was sung by the martyrs in 1886 as they went to their death. All the bishops - except Festo Kivengere, who had been warned that he was the next target, and had already left for his home diocese - stood on the cathedral steps, and Dunstan, Bishop of that Cathedral, called out to us:

"They may kill us all but the church will never die. Stand firm in the faith."

The hymn started up again. The grave stood empty. The spies in the crowd stood open-mouthed, quite unable to comprehend the joyful singing of thousands of people, who had lost their archbishop, been refused his body for burial, and were standing there in danger of their lives.

The church was celebrating another martyr. It was the most exciting funeral.

Other state funerals tended to be endurance tests, and I was often relieved when I couldn't get a seat: outside you could walk about a bit and even go away for a snack; but one I was inside for I shall never forget.

John Wilson - a Ugandan despite his name - was one of the very first people to come back into Uganda after the liberation from Amin's Regime in 1979, and a few years later he was back in Kampala running a mission to the People of Kampala called GOD LOVES KAMPALA. For reasons that were never made clear, his car was held up quite near the cathedral and he was shot at close range in front of witnesses. He died a few minutes later. John's family were scattered all over the world, and they came from Britain and America and took part in his funeral, reading the lessons and testifying to the love of God and their forgiveness of those who had so senselessly killed their father. One son said he had flown in from Los Angeles full of bitter anger and it could explode into words; but instead he would say to each member of the family what John would have said. Very faithfully he did just that, and a tremendous load of grief seemed to be lifted as he spoke, because it was as if John were still there. There were several sermons, one by a Kenyan bishop, and one by Michael Cassidy, who spoke on three Why's, exploring the agony of what had happened and ending with Jesus' question to Judas: "Why are you here, friend?" He said there were some Judases in the congregation, but he was not referring to the - very likely - presence of government spies, but to those who were God's enemies, standing there in church to attend a funeral, but caring nothing for God. He had worked for Evangelistic Enterprise, and colleagues came from all over Africa to be there. Bishop Festo Kivengere preached his sermon on:

> All things are yours,
> And you are Christ's
> And Christ is God's

He said the bullet had not deprived John of anything - life, time, death, for he was not possessed by them, he now possessed them all in Christ.

Here was a man whose life had been threatened by Amin preaching forgiveness for a friend and colleague whose life had now been taken under the next regime - Obote's. But the message of reconciliation was there for all to hear, and it was said afterwards:

"He died for Kampala."

The words seemed to echo those of Bishop Hannington so many years before. The message he sent to King Muwanga that dark day in October 1885 was:

TELL THE KING I HAVE BOUGHT THE ROAD TO BUGANDA WITH MY LIFE.

Somehow funerals in Uganda remind me of a comment once made about Jesus himself, that he broke up every funeral he attended. Of course he did, seeing he is the Resurrection and the Life. Some of his disciples in Uganda have come very near to doing the same.

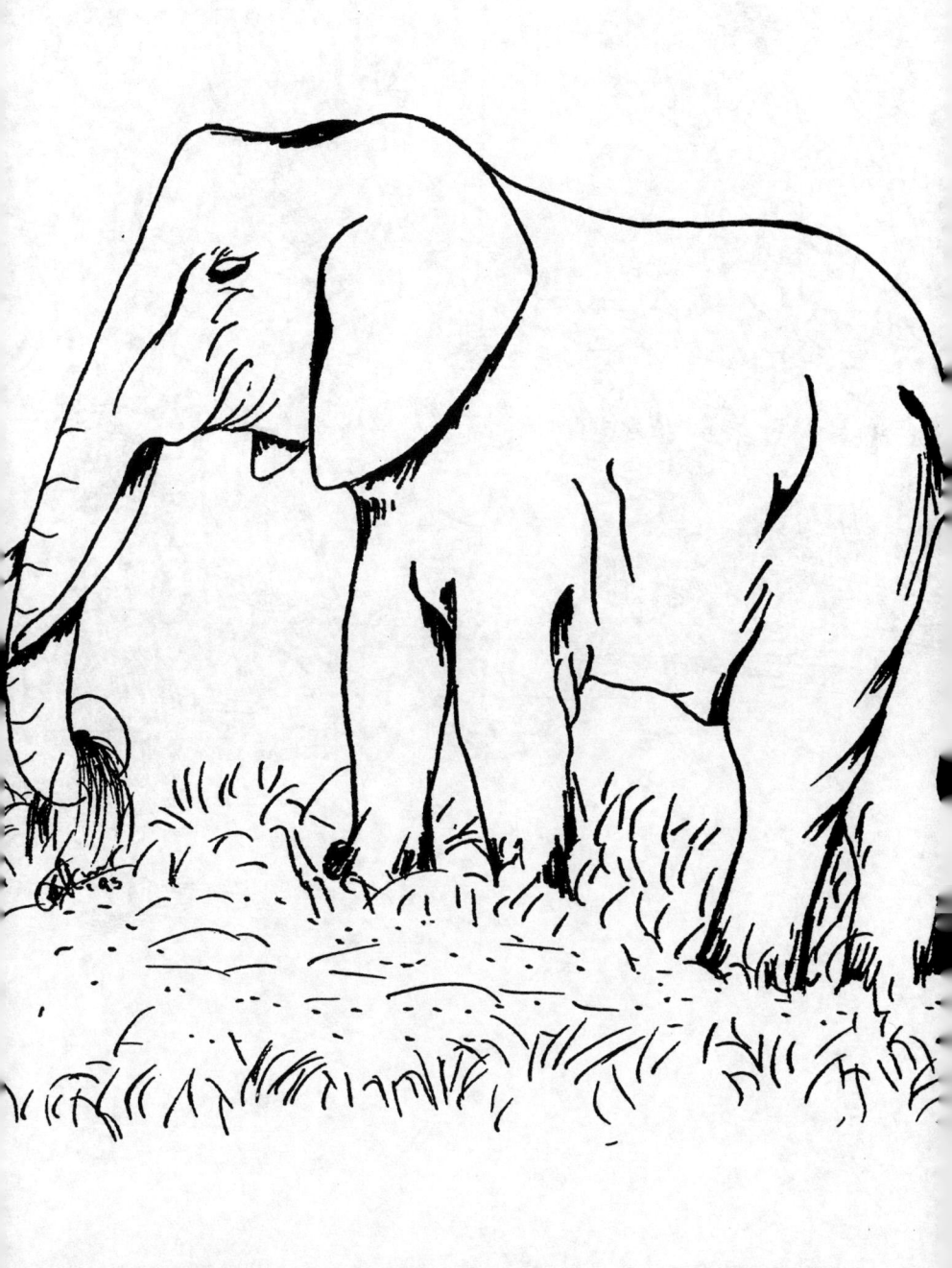

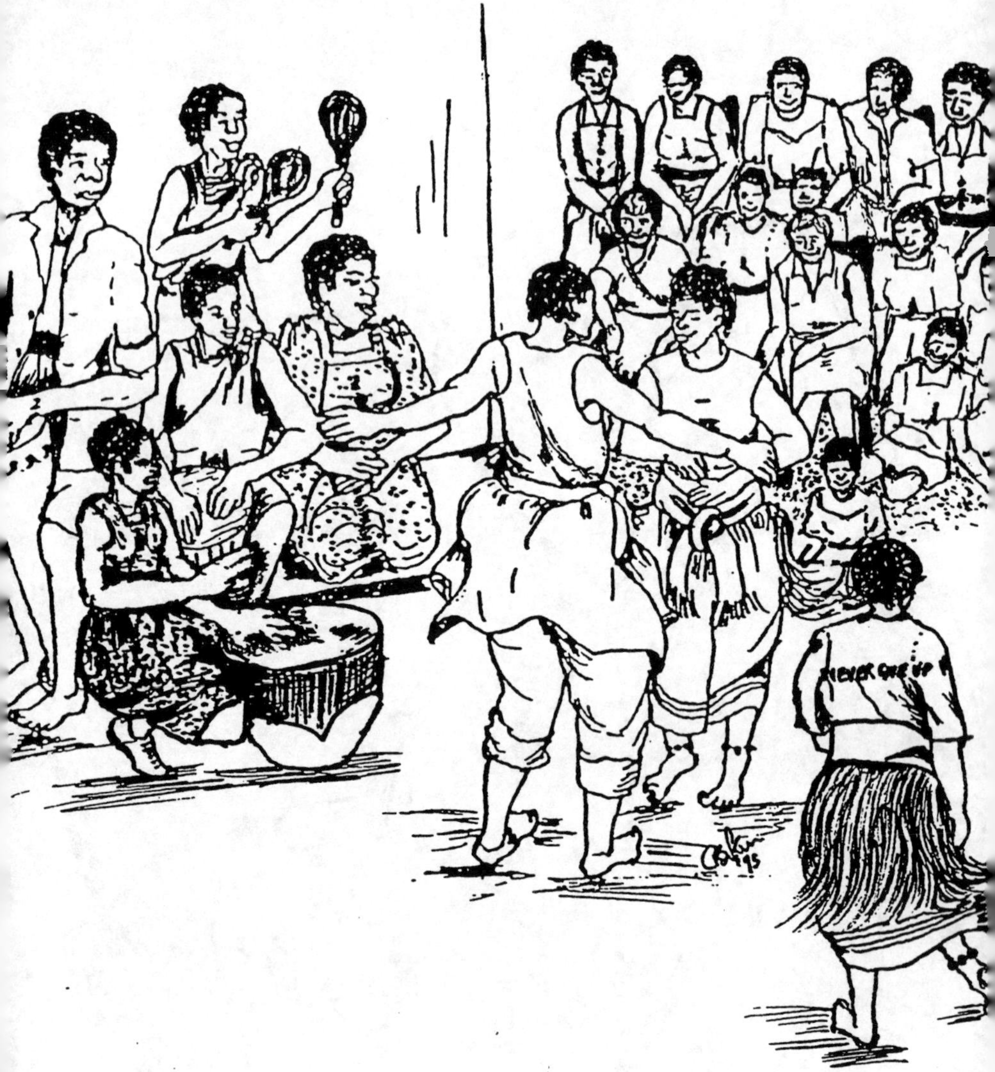

10. MY CUP OVERFLOWS

When I left Uganda in 1990, it was still struggling economically, still beset by guerrilla activity, still coming to terms with the scourge of Aids. But somehow even these problems led to good - for the high prices and fees meant that people had to learn to share; the continuing fighting meant that they were always reminded that the opinions of others matter and dictatorship is out; and the need to face the realities of the causes and consequences of Aids made everyone look at their lifestyle and seek some way of relieving those who suffered from Aids or as a result of losing their partners or parents. Compassion has to grow in such circumstances.

I handed over my school to its first Ugandan head in April 1990 and went off to Kenya for the first local holiday for ten years, returning to produce 'The Merchant of Venice', a set book, with the sixth form, in between packing and saying goodbye all round. It had been twenty years since I had had time to produce Shakespeare, and I found the girls were not used to my demands and expectations. But we managed to do it in a month, although both the Duke and the wardrobe mistress got typhoid just as the play was due.

All sorts of families and organisations began to throw parties and make presentations, and we held the first ever Old Girls' Day at the school, later to become a regular fixture for June. I was ill with malaria that day and could only stagger out for photos and speeches in the afternoon, but it was a very happy occasion and brought back memories of the early days.

My last weekend was unforgettable. The school put on a day-long concert, in which every class and club performed plays, songs and dances in English and vernacular languages, in costumes from all over the world and on topics ranging from family comedy to international espionage. There was a pause midday for lunch when I alone went to share a meal with the girls in the dining room. I was no stranger there as I usually went to lunch every Monday. But this was a feast. By serving the food outside and seating the younger ones on the floor, all 665 girls were squeezed in. I was given some lovely presents, all Ugandan, and perhaps the most treasured is a busuuti, the national ladies' costume, hand-printed in tie-and-dye by the art group, using all the colours and made in the same material as the school uniform dresses. Goodness knows how many hours of toil, trial and error it represents. I changed into it for the second part of the concert, after tea, and to their huge delight I joined in the final Kiga dance, somewhat impeded by the long skirt. The audio tape of the performance reminds me of the howls of mirth which greeted this item. The video had run out by then.

So ended Saturday. On Sunday I preached my last sermon in the chapel and was entertained to elevenses once more in the "DR", this time with the staff as well, and there were all the Christian songs they had not yet performed and a vast white cake, at least two feet long which meant that everyone got a piece. I had to rush away from that with the head girl, to lunch with the Minister of Education. Here again I came away loaded with gifts and kind words.

With four days left I began to pack and dispose of my possessions. Every last pencil stub and old mat was snapped up by someone, and the three hundred kilogram luggage allowance from the British Government went off full of presents, little else. I had no means of weighing it, and no help with packing; but all arrived intact, and on arrival in UK the weigh bill showed

297 kilograms. I could only marvel.

The last party of all was with the staff and was very moving. There were comic songs and the hilarious sight of the music teacher, who is English, dressed in a grass skirt and performing the local royal dance with some of the young men. Neither are normally seen in such costume! The song at the beginning of the book was one of their offerings, showing a remarkable insight and sympathy with the trials of a headteacher. They would not have been so understanding twenty years earlier.

Leaving a job like that after umpteen years is a real bereavement experience, but the love and warmth of those celebrations kept me going through the bleak months that followed. Escorted by a lorry load of girls and a bus full of staff, I finally left from the airport on the Friday morning, though we had a puncture on the way there as if to remind me that life would go on much the same as I had known it.

And it did: water shortages, electricity cuts, rising prices and deaths from Aids continued, and there was still no sign of peace in the North and East of the country even two years later. But hope shines on and my overriding impressions of Uganda remain unchanged. It remains a place of brilliant colours and great beauty; a place where you think you have summed up the weather, only to find it playing dangerous tricks, blowing off roofs or scorching your crops. It is a place above all of a people who are resilient and resourceful; people who must be brilliant considering what they achieve often without books or teachers; people who never give up in the face of poverty, sickness, danger or persecution, bereavement or any form of apparent impossibility. They sing, they dance, they celebrate; they welcome strangers with abundant hospitality. They enjoy life, whatever it brings.

People still say when you mention Uganda: "Oh, Amin's

place." And I reply as always, "No, God's place", God's country: God's beloved country.

After teaching there for thirty-three years, I ask myself: what did I teach them? I think I could claim to have taught them a good deal about the use of words, not least in poetry, my special love. I tried to teach them to look at the glory around them, to concern themselves with justice, especially for the underdogs. I tried to teach them to persevere, to reach their full potential, to "never give up." In my role as confirmation class teacher and headmistress, I think I passed on a trust in God and an assurance of eternal life. I think I encouraged them to go out from school believing that what they did mattered, and that they mattered to God.

And what did I learn from them and life there? First, patience. You had to learn patience with things, circumstances, people, or go away. It took years, but it happened. Then I learnt to receive the generosity of people who had nothing and gave everything, an experience which completely alters your perspective and values, so that you come to see that the spirit of giving is far more important than the material value. I remember an auction where a gas stove went for a song, and a pineapple for thousands. They did not want to take home value for money: they wanted to give to a cause they believed in. I learnt the importance of celebrating whenever possible whatever possible, and weddings and farewell suppers became a delight. I thought I had learnt to do without thanks, for everything was always "their" fault and most of the time the head represented "them". But after the amazing farewell parties and gifts I received I could no longer say that!

Above all I learnt from Ugandan Christians the power of praise. Some used to sing a song with the refrain, "Alleluia, anyhow", and it was typical of the attitude that I came to realise was truly Christian. "We are going on whatever may come our way," was one level. "Alleluia anyhow", was another, and they really meant it. You could think when people greeted you with "Praise God" that it was a hackneyed phrase of little meaning or a trick phrase to find out if you belonged to their religious group; but after hearing it for years on the lips of people who have suffered and gone on smiling, I came to realise that it is a deeply spiritual approach to life and all it brings:

TUKUTENDEREZA : PRAISE THE LORD

Being at "home" after all those years is very much like exile, and also a bit like being a grannie, for photos come labelled "your grandson", which means I taught the mother at one time. But life goes on, and one of the joys is the constant supply of photos showing one's staff and old girls graduating or getting married; the babies and toddlers growing up into schoolboys and girls; new buildings appearing - even if they are just houses for generators rather than for teachers. You see trees growing taller, wild patches being cleared, fatter cows on the farm. At the same time you see the same old chairs out on the grass for concerts, the same roofs in need of repair, the same uniforms - only the wearers are different. And you know that it all goes on as ever, which is reassuring. Best of all, you meet in the UK the results of past years of training, in the shape of students reading for second degrees in Britain, so happy to reminisce, and to tell you freely what it meant to belong to their school. And every week there are letters on the mat, full of tales, joys and sorrows, successes and problems, and you realise with relief rather than regret that while you can share in the delights and the anxieties,

you don't have to solve the problems any longer.
But Africa steals the hearts of those who live there.
So be it.

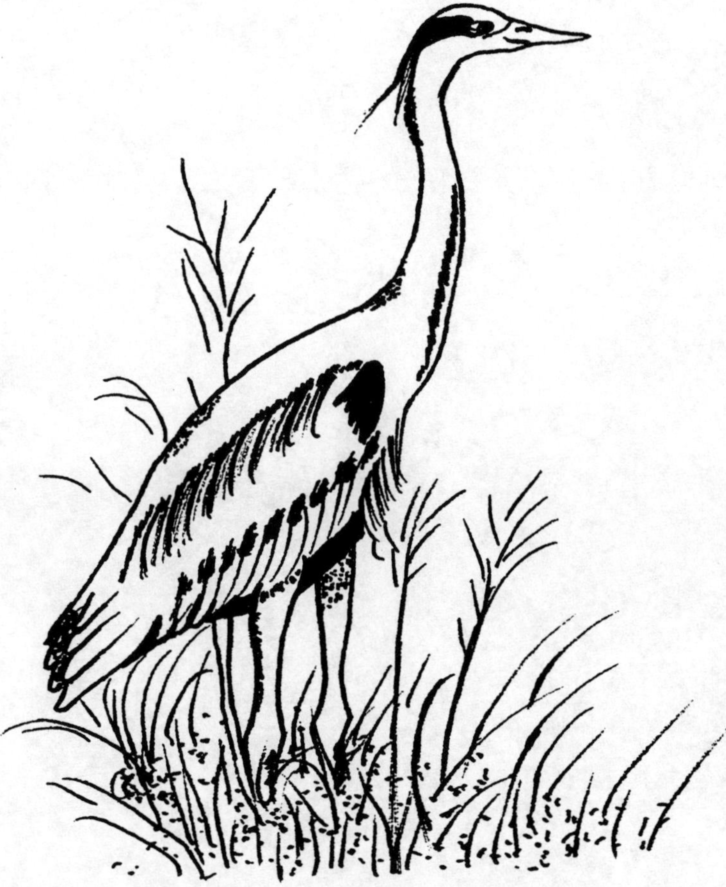